COMPANION TO THE QUMRAN SCROLLS
9

Editor
Philip R. Davies

Published under
LIBRARY OF SECOND TEMPLE STUDIES
62

formerly the Journal for the Study of the Pseudepigrapha Supplement Series

Editor
Lester L. Grabbe

THE SEREKH TEXTS

Sarianna Metso

t&t clark

Published by T&T Clark International
A Continuum imprint
The Tower Building, 11 York Road, London SE1 7NX
80 Maiden Lane, Suite 704, New York, NY 10038

www.tandtclark.com

British Library Cataloguing-in-Publication Data
A catalogue record for this book is available from the British Library

ISBN-10: 0-567-04092-5   (hardback)
ISBN-13: 978-0-567-04092-3   (hardback)

Typeset by ISB Typesetting, Sheffield
Printed on acid-free paper in Great Britain by Biddles Ltd, King's Lynn, Norfolk

For Gene

CONTENTS

ABBREVIATIONS

BASOR	*Bulletin of the American Schools of Oriental Research*
BJS	Brown Judaic Studies
BO	*Bibliotheca orientalis*
CRINT	Compendia rerum iudaicarum ad Novum Testamentum
DBSup	*Dictionnaire de la Bible: Supplément* (ed. L. Pirot and A. Robert; Paris , 1928–)
DJD	Discoveries in the Judaean Desert
DJDJ	Discoveries in the Judaean Desert of Jordan
DSD	*Dead Sea Discoveries*
JBL	*Journal of Biblical Literature*
JJS	*Journal of Jewish Studies*
JSJ	*Journal for the Study of Judaism in the Persian, Hellenistic, and Roman Periods*
JSJSup	*Journal for the Study of Judaism in the Persian, Hellenistic , and Roman Periods*, Supplement Series
JSNTSup	*Journal for the Study of the New Testament*, Supplement Series
JSOTSup	*Journal for the Study of the Old Testament*, Supplement Series
JSP	*Journal for the Study of the Pseudepigrapha*
JSPSup	*Journal for the Study of the Pseudepigrapha*, Supplement Series
JSS	*Journal of Semitic Studies*
LXX	Septuagint
MT	Masoretic Text
NTOA	Novum Testamentum et Orbis Antiquus
NTS	*New Testament Studies*
RB	*Revue biblique*
RevQ	*Revue de Qumran*
RHR	*Revue de l'histoire des religions*
SBT	Studies in Biblical Theology
SJLA	Studies in Judaism in Late Antiquity
SNTSMS	Society for New Testament Studies Monograph Series
SPB	Studia post-biblica
SSEJC	Studies in Scripture in Early Judaism and Christianity
ST	*Studia Theologica*
STDJ	Studies on the Texts of the Desert of Judah
SUNT	Studien zur Umwelt des Neuen Testaments
ThWAT	*Theologische Wörterbuch zum Alten Testament* (ed. G. J. Botterweck and H. Ringgren; Stuttgart, 1970–)
Tru	*Theologische Rundschau*
VTSup	Vetus Testamentum Supplements
WUNT	Wissenschaftliche Untersuchungen zum Alten und Neuen Testament
ZTK	*Zeitschrift für Theologie und Kirche*

EDITIONS, TRANSLATIONS AND BIBLIOGRAPHIES

Editions of 1QS

Burrows, M. with J. C. Trever, W. H. Brownlee, *The Dead Sea Scrolls of St. Mark's Monastery. Vol. II, Fasc. 2. Plates and Transcription of the Manual of Discipline* (New Haven: The American Schools of Oriental Research, 1951).

Cross, F. M., D. N. Freedman, and J. A. Sanders (eds), *Scrolls from Qumran Cave I: The Great Isaiah Scroll, the Order of the Community, the Pesher to Habakkuk, from Photographs by J. C. Trever* (Jerusalem: Shrine of the Book, 1972).

Habermann, A. M., *Megilloth Midbar Yehudah: The Scrolls from the Judaean Desert, Edited with Vocalization, Introduction, Notes and Concordance* (Jerusalem: Machbaroth Lesifruth, 1959), pp. 60–70.

Licht, J., *Megillat has-Serakim: The Rule Scroll: A Scroll from the Wilderness of Judaea: 1QS, 1QSa, 1QSb: Text, Introduction and Commentary* (Jerusalem: Bialik Institute, 1965).

Lohse, E., *Die Texte aus Qumran: Hebräisch und Deutsch, mit Masoretischer Punktation, Übersetzung, Einführung und Anmerkungen* (Munich: Kösel-Verlag, 4th edn, 1986).

Martone, C., *La 'Regola della Comunità': Edizione critica* (Quaderni di Henoch 8; Torino: Silvio Zamorani Editore, 1995).

Qimron, E., 'The Community Rule', in *The Dead Sea Scrolls* (supervised by M. Sekine; Tokyo: Kodansha, 1979), pp. 112–32.

Qimron, E., and J. H. Charlesworth, 'Rule of the Community (1QS)', in J. H. Charlesworth *et al.* (eds), *The Dead Sea Scrolls: Hebrew, Aramaic, and Greek Texts with English Translations*, vol. 1: *Rule of the Community and Related Documents* (Tübingen: J. C. B. Mohr [Paul Siebeck]; Louisville, KY: Westminster John Knox Press, 1994), pp. 1–51.

Preliminary Descriptions of Cave 4 Fragments

Alexander, P. S., 'The Redaction History of Serekh Ha-Yaḥad: A Proposal', *RevQ* 17 (1996), pp. 437–56.

Hempel, C., 'Comments on the Translation of 4QS^d I,1', *JJS* 44 (1993), pp. 127–28.

Metso, S., 'The Primary Results of the Reconstruction of 4QS^e', *JJS 44* (1993), pp. 303–308.

—*The Textual Development of the Qumran Community Rule* (STDJ, 21; Leiden: Brill, 1997).

Milik, J. T., 'Le travail d'édition des fragments manuscrits de Qumran', *RB* 63 (1956), pp. 4–67.

—'Texte des variantes des dix manuscrits de la Règle de la Communauté trouvés dans la Grotte 4: Recension de P.Wernberg-Moeller, The Manual of Discipline', *RB* 67 (1960), pp. 410–16.

—'Milkî-ṣedeq et Milkî-reša' dans les anciens écrits juifs et chrétiens', *JJS* 23 (1972), pp. 95–144, esp. p. 135.

—'Numérotation des feuilles des rouleaux dans le scriptorium de Qumrân (Planches X et XI)', *Semitica* 27 (1977), pp. 75–81.

Vermes, G., 'Preliminary Remarks on Unpublished Fragments of the Community Rule from Qumran Cave 4', *JJS* 42 (1991), pp. 250–55.

Editions of Cave 4 Fragments

Alexander, P. S., and G. Vermes, *Qumran Cave 4,XIX: Serekh ha-Yaḥad and Two Related Texts*, (DJD, 26; Oxford: Clarendon Press, 1998).

Qimron, E., and J. H. Charlesworth, with an Appendix by F. M. Cross, 'Cave IV Fragments (4Q255–264 = 4QS MSS A–J)', in J. H. Charlesworth *et al.* (eds), *The Dead Sea Scrolls: Hebrew, Aramaic, and Greek Texts with English Translations.* I. *Rule of the Community and Related Documents* (Tübingen: J. C. B. Mohr [Paul Siebeck]; Louisville, KY: Westminster John Knox Press, 1994), pp. 53–103.

Editions of 5Q11

Charlesworth, J. H., 'Possible Fragment of the Rule of the Community (5Q11)', in J. H. Charlesworth *et al.* (eds), *The Dead Sea Scrolls: Hebrew, Aramaic, and Greek Texts with English Translations.* I. *Rule of the Community and Related Documents* (Tübingen: J. C. B. Mohr [Paul Siebeck]; Louisville, KY: Westminster John Knox Press, 1994), pp. 105–107.

Milik, J. T., '5Q11. Règle de la Communauté', in M. Baillet, J. T. Milik, and R. de Vaux , *Les 'Petites Grottes' de Qumrân* (DJD, 3; Oxford: Clarendon Press, 1962), pp. 180–81 + pl. XXXVIII.

Possible Fragment of S from Cave 11

García Martínez, F., E. J. C. Tigchelaar and A. S. van der Woude, '29. 11QFragment Related to Serekh ha-Yaḥad', in *Qumran Cave 11.II: 11Q2–18, 11Q20–31* (DJD, 23; Oxford: Clarendon Press, 1998), pp. 433–34 + pl. L.

Tigchelaar, E. J. C., 'A Newly Identified 11QSerekh ha-Yaḥad Fragment (11Q29)?', in L.H. Schiffman, E. Tov, and J. C. VanderKam (eds), *The Dead Sea Scrolls: Fifty Years After Their Discovery. Proceedings of the Jerusalem Congress, July 20–25, 1997* (Jerusalem: Israel Exploration Society in cooperation with the Shrine of the Book, Israel Museum, 2000), pp. 285–92.

Translations

Charlesworth, J. H. *et al.* (eds), *The Dead Sea Scrolls: Photographic Multi-Language Edition* (Philadelphia: American Interfaith Institute / World Alliance, 1996).

García Martínez, F., *The Dead Sea Scrolls Translated: The Qumran Texts in English* (trans. W. G. E. Watson; Leiden: Brill, 1994).

Guilbert, P., 'La Règle de la Communauté', in J. Carmignac and P. Guilbert, *Les Textes de Qumran traduits et annotés*, vol. 1(Paris: Letouzey et Ané, 1961), pp. 9–80.

Knibb, M. A., *The Qumran Community* (Cambridge Commentaries on Writings of the Jewish and Christian World 200 BC to AD 200, 2; Cambridge: Cambridge University Press, 1987).

Leaney, A. R. C., *The Rule of Qumran and Its Meaning: Introduction, Translation and Commentary* (London: SCM Press, 1966).

Vermes, G., *The Complete Dead Sea Scrolls in English* (London: Penguin Books, rev. edn, 2004).

Wernberg-Møller, P., *The Manual of Discipline Translated and Annotated with an Introduction* (STDJ, 1; Leiden: Brill, 1957).

Wise, M., M. Abegg Jr, and E. Cook, *The Dead Sea Scrolls: A New Translation* (San Francisco: HarperSanFrancisco, 1996).

Study Editions with Translations

García Martínez, F. and E. J. C. Tigchelaar (eds), *The Dead Sea Scrolls Study Edition* (2 vols.; Leiden: Brill, 1997–98).

Parry, D. W., and E. Tov (eds), *Texts Concerned with Religious Law* (The Dead Sea Scrolls Reader, 1; Leiden: Brill, 2004).

Bibliographies

Bardtke, H., 'Literaturbericht über Qumran. VII Teil', *TRu* 38 (1974), pp. 256–91.

The Dead Sea Scrolls Electronic Bibliography at the Orion Center of the Hebrew University of Jerusalem: http://orion.mscc.huji.ac.il/

Gagnon, R. A., 'How did the Rule of the Community Obtain its Final Shape? A Review of Scholarly Research', *JSP* 10 (1992), pp. 61–79.

Fitzmyer, J. A., *The Dead Sea Scrolls and Major Publications for Study* (SBL Resources for Biblical Study, 20; Atlanta: Scholars Press, 1990).

Jongeling, B., *A Classified Bibliography of the Finds in the Desert of Judah 1958–1969* (STDJ, 7; Leiden: Brill, 1971).

Pinnick, A., *The Orion Center Bibliography of the Dead Sea Scrolls (1995–2000)* (STDJ, 41; Leiden: Brill, 2001).

Chapter 1

INTRODUCTION

Discovery and Publication

It was largely because of the Community Rule (1QS) that the manuscripts discovered at Qumran were able to be identified as belonging to the Essenes, although the name Essene is used nowhere in the Scrolls. Providing a set of regulations dealing with the practices and teachings of the community, this writing bears striking similarities to the description of the Essenes found in the writings of Josephus, a Jewish historian of the late first century. The parallels between 1QS and Josephus number over thirty, among them detailed descriptions of the procedure of entry into the community, the pooling of wealth, strict hierarchical order, common meals, and ritual washings.

The Community Rule was one of the first seven scrolls found in Cave 1 in 1947. This manuscript consisting of eleven columns is almost complete, and it was soon published by M. Burrows under the title 'Manual of Discipline' (1951). The opening lines of the manuscript, however, bear the title *Serekh ha-yaḥad*, i.e. the Community Rule, and it is by this name that the work is now known. Copied on the same scroll with the Community Rule were two other works, the Rule of the Congregation (1QSa) and the Blessings (1QSb).

When Cave 4 was discovered in 1952, fragments of ten other manuscripts of the Community Rule were also found there. Although the first partial report of the variants included in the fragments was issued as early as 1956 by J. T. Milik, and other preliminary discussions and editions followed (Qimron, Charlesworth and Cross 1994: 53–103; Vermes 1991: 250–55; Alexander 1996: 437–56; Metso 1997) the critical edition of 4QS^{a-j} remained unpublished until the 1990s. In 1998, P. Alexander and G. Vermes published the ten manuscripts in vol. 26 of Discoveries of the Judaean Desert, and although the discussion on these manuscripts is still in its early stages, it is already clear that they display considerable differences in comparison with 1QS.

In Cave 5, two more tiny fragments surviving from yet a twelfth manuscript of the Community Rule (5Q11) were found (Milik 1962: 180–81), and more recently from Cave 11, a fragment (11Q29) most likely belonging to a thirteenth manuscript was identified (Tigchelaar 2000: 285–92). Additional fragments surfaced of a manuscript entitled simply the Rule (5Q13) that quotes a phrase from the Community Rule. Sections of the Community Rule are also quoted in Cave 4 manuscripts of the Damascus Document (4Q266 frg. 10 and 4Q270 frg. 7), the Miscellaneous Rules (4Q265; formerly Serekh Dameseq), and possibly the Ritual of Marriage (4Q502 frg. 16). Other manuscripts related to the Community Rule are Rebukes Reported by the Overseer (4Q477; formerly Decrees), Communal Ceremony (4Q275), and Four Lots (4Q279).

The Community Rule has added new evidence and increased understanding in many areas. It has played a central role in reconstructions of the history of the life of the Qumran Community and the wider Essene movement. It has also been an important source for the linguistic study of ancient Hebrew as well as for the study of scribal practices of that period. The way biblical quotations were used and the forms of community life depicted in the Community Rule have remarkable similarities to those in the New Testament Gospels and Letters. The document provides also a fascinating window into theological developments of the turn of the era, such as eschatology and messianism, predestination, and ideas of justification.

Physical Descriptions

1QS

The manuscript from Cave 1 (1QS) is the best preserved of all the copies of the Community Rule. It consists of five leather sheets stitched together, containing eleven columns, each of which has approximately 26 lines (the following text of 1QSa begins with a new sheet). The length of 1QS is approximately 187 cm (approx. 6' 2''). The manuscript has only a few gaps, located in the lower edges of columns, but there are many textual errors, corrections, glosses and marks in the margins, especially in columns VII and VIII. Interestingly, the scribe who copied 1QS also copied 4QSam^c and 4QTestimonia (Ulrich 1979: 1–25; 2002: 187–90).

Two other documents, the Rule of the Congregation (1QSa) and Words of Blessing (1QSb), were copied on the same scroll by the same scribe, and parts of seven columns survive. These compositions have been preserved only fragmentarily, for they were written on the outer layers of the scroll. Since the scroll was rolled with the beginning of the text on the inside, it is impossible to say from the material evidence whether the originally combined scroll consisted of more than the eighteen columns which have been preserved. The length of the preserved parts of the scroll is about three meters. The scroll of 1QS, 1QSa and 1QSb has been dated on palaeographical grounds to 100–75 BCE, and radio-carbon tests confirm this dating (Bonani *et al.* 1991: 27–32).

On the verso of the handle sheet belonging to the beginning of 1QS, there is a line written vertically across the scroll. This line contained the title of the scroll. Eight letters are preserved, and the first word can easily be completed: [סרך] היחד ומן. The words סרך היחד presumably refer to the text of 1QS I–XI, whereas ומן should probably be understood as beginning that part of the title which referred to 1QSa and 1QSb. Manuscripts 4QS^a and 4QS^c have partly preserved the same title as 1QS, and they also indicate that the word ומן did not belong to the title of the Community Rule (apart from 1QSa and 1QSb).

The scribe(s) of 1QS used two basic techniques for indicating sections within the text: blank spaces and marks in the margin. An intentional space, or interval, often appears in connection with an introductory formula, but smaller intervals also precede smaller breaks in the text. A blank space, however, does not always signify the beginning of a new section. Presumably sometimes the 'model manuscript' (*Vorlage*) which the copyist of 1QS was using was in some places so poorly preserved that he was unable to read it properly and thus left the problematic places blank. Some spaces in columns VII and VIII were probably caused by the poor condition of the *Vorlage*. Some of them were later filled in by the second scribe, but by omitting some of the words written by the first scribe he also created further intervals in the text. In column VII (after line 7) there is an unusually large space of nearly three lines, but it was caused by a defect in the leather, as also in the case of VI.10; IX.9,14 and 16.

The manuscript has two kinds of marks in the right margin. First, a paragraphos, usually a horizontal line with a small hook (similar to cryptic *'ayin*), appears either by itself or in conjunction with a space to mark the end of a section or of an important sentence or paragraph. Secondly, large signs, composed of palaeo-Hebrew letters, were drawn in the margins of columns V, VII, and IX to mark sections of particular importance (for fuller discussion, see Tov 2004: 178–218).

4QpapS^a (4Q255)

The text of 4QS^a was written on one side of a papyrus manuscript whose other side is inscribed with 4QpapHodayot-like Text B (4Q433a) (Schuller 1999: 237). It has been preserved in four fragments, but only two of them provide clear parallels to 1QS. Fragment 1 has preserved parts of six lines from the upper left corner of column I. These lines are parallel to 1QS I.1–5 and partly supply the few words lost at the beginning of 1QS. Fragment 2 is the largest with nine almost complete lines from the upper right corner of a column. The fragment provides a parallel to 1QS III.7–12. Fragment 3 (named 'A' by Alexander and Vermes 1998) is a piece from a lower left corner. There is no direct parallel in 1QS to the five lines of this fragment, but the vocabulary is similar to the treatise on the two spirits (1QS III.13–IV.26). There is a slight possibility that fragment 3 forms a loose parallel to 1QS III.20–25. Fragment 4 (named 'B' by Alexander and Vermes) has preserved only a few letters from the right edge of a column, but no recognizable word or part of a word which could help to identify the fragment. According to Cross, this manuscript, written in a crude cursive script, dates from the second half of the second century BCE, probably from the end of that century.

4QS^b (4Q256)

Fifteen fragments of this manuscript, grouped as 4QS^b frgs 1–8 by Alexander and Vermes, have been preserved, and they provide parallel passages for all the main sections of 1QS except for the treatise on the two spirits (1QS III.13–IV.26). The version of the Community Rule preserved in 4QS^b is much shorter than the one in 1QS, however. This is shown especially by frgs 4 (shorter parallel to 1QS V.1–20) and 5a–6 (shorter parallel to 1QS VI.10–13). According to Milik (1977: 76–78 [4QS^b was formerly called 4QS^d]), the manuscript belongs to the transitional period between the Hasmonean and Herodian script, and is to be dated to 50–25 BCE. Cross (1994: 57) states that it represents the typical early Herodian Formal script of c. 30–1 BCE. The manuscript can be reconstructed only partially. The measurements of several columns can be calculated, however, and with the information provided by the parallel manuscript 4QS^d it can be estimated that the text of the Community Rule in 4QS^b consisted of twenty (Metso 1997: 24) to twenty-three (Alexander and Vermes 1998: 39) columns. The text corresponding to the end of the manuscript 1QS (XI.22) has been preserved in 4QS^b, but interestingly, the words that form the end of 1QS are followed in 4QS^b by additional material, either a final formula or the beginning of another text.

4QSpap^c (4Q257)
Like 4QS^a, manuscript 4QS^c is written on papyrus with writing on both sides. The text of the Community Rule is on the recto. A couple of words are written on the verso, but the text cannot be identified. Cross (1994: 57) has dated the manuscript to c. 100–75 BCE, i.e. roughly to the same period when 1QS was copied. Except for a minute piece difficult to identify and some features of orthography and grammar, the text of 4QS^c in the preserved parts is practically identical with that in 1QS. The eight pieces preserved of 4QS^c provide parallels to parts of 1QS I–IV.

4QS^d (4Q258)
The most sizeable fragments from the Cave 4 copies of the Rule belong to the manuscript known as 4QS^d. The individual columns of this manuscript are remarkably small, however. The original size of a single column was no more than about 10.7 cm wide by 8.0 cm high with only 13–14 lines. The script used in the manuscript is Herodian and dates from the last third of the last century BCE (Cross 1994: 57). The name of God (אל) is written in palaeo-Hebrew letters in col. VIII.9 and col. IX.8. The beginning of column I of fragment 1 was most likely also the beginning of the whole manuscript: the margin at the right edge of the manuscript is unusually wide (2.1 cm) compared to the other margins (0.9–1.2 cm), and there are no marks of stitching at the right edge of the leather sheet. The beginning of the text corresponds to 1QS V.1. That is, it lacks the first four columns of 1QS: the introduction (1QS I.1–18a), the liturgical passage (I.18b– III.12) and the treatise on the two spirits (III.13–IV.26). The absence of 1QS I–IV turns out to be not so surprising, however, for the Rule is comprised of diverse component sections and the contents of columns 1QS I–IV are quite different from those of V–XI. The actual regulations for community life begin only with column 1QS V. The text of 4QS^d is similar to that of 4QS^b in witnessing to a shorter version of the material in 1QS columns V–VII. Material reconstruction of the manuscripts helps demonstrate this shorter, and presumably earlier, edition of the text (see Chapter 3 for fuller discussion).

4QS^e (4Q259)
4QS^e preserves fragments from four columns, all from the latter part of the Community Rule (par. 1QS VII–IX); it is unclear whether the material of 1QS I–IV was included in this manuscript. The manuscript displays interesting differences compared to 1QS: 4QS^e col. III lacks a long passage that would have provided a

parallel to 1QS VIII.15b–IX.11, and 4QS^e col. IV included a calendrical text, 4QOtot, instead of the final psalm in 1QS X–XI. Milik dated the manuscript to the second half of the second century BCE (he labeled this manuscript '4QS^b' and the attached calendrical text the 'Book of Signs' or 'ha-'Ôtot' [1976: 61–64]), but according to F. M. Cross the paleographical date of this manuscript should be placed c. 50–25 BCE.

4QS^f (4Q260)
Seven fragments (for one of which no PAM photo exists) containing the upper part of five columns survive from the early Herodian manuscript 4QS^f. They provide material parallel to parts of 1QS IX–X. There are some orthographical and grammatical variants as well as variants of content in this manuscript, but the preserved material is not sufficient to make any general assessment of its relationship to 1QS.

4QS^g (4Q261)
Nineteen small fragments, many of them less than 1 sq. cm in size, remain of 4QS^g. According to Cross (1994: 57), the script of the manuscript is semicursive and dates to c. 50–1 BCE. Due to the poor condition of the material, it is very difficult to read and identify many of the fragments. Those that can be identified, provide parallels to 1QS V–VII, displaying a text that is sometimes shorter and at other times longer than that of 1QS.

4QS^h (4Q262)
Only two fragments can be confidently identified as belonging to the manuscript labeled as 4QS^h. Fragment 1 alone has a parallel in 1QS (1QS III.4–6), whereas no parallel can be identified for fragments 2 and 3 (named A and B by Alexander and Vermes). There is a good likelihood that the manuscript is not a copy of the Community Rule at all, but some other work (a collection of hymns?) quoting a phrase from the Community Rule. Interestingly, the text in fragment 1 is the same as that cited in manuscript 5Q13. According to Cross (1994: 57), the script of 4QS^h is vulgar semiformal and dates to about the first half of the first century CE.

4QS^i (4Q263)
Only one fragment 4.1 cm × 3.6 cm in size is preserved of this early Herodian manuscript (30–1 BCE; Cross 1994: 57). It provides a parallel to 1QS VI.1–4.

4QS^j (4Q264)
Only one fragment (4.4 cm × 4.3 cm) is left of this manuscript as well, dating from the second half of the first century BCE (Cross 1994: 57). The fragment provides a parallel to the last lines of the Cave 1 copy of the Community Rule (1QS XI.14–22). The left edge of the fragment, however, has marks of stitching. The sheet that followed may have been a handle sheet, if the scroll ended with the text of the Community Rule. Alternatively, another text may have followed, but it is unknown whether it would have been the Rule of the Congregation as in the scroll of 1QS, or some other, unidentifiable text as in the scroll of 4QS^b.

5QS (5Q11)

One fragment of a Herodian copy of the Community Rule has been found in Cave 5. The size of the fragment is only 3.1 cm × 4.8 cm, and it has preserved parts of six lines from two contiguous columns with stitching in the middle. Only the column on the right side, which forms a parallel to 1QS II.4–7, can be identified with certainty. On the edge of the left column, remains of only about six letters are recognizable. Milik (1962: 181) suggests that they correspond to 1QS II.12–14. If his identification is correct, and if the text in the unpreserved part of column I followed 1QS, there were fourteen lines per column in this manuscript. Filling up the lines of the fragment with the aid of 1QS reveals that there were differences between the two manuscripts, omissions and additions.

11QFragment Related to Serekh ha-Yaḥad (11Q29)

One of the tiny fragments from Cave 11, with only parts of two lines extant, contains a parallel, albeit with a variant, to the text of 1QS VII.18–19. The fragment may represent a copy of the Community Rule, or alternatively, a different manuscript with a penal code, comparable to the penal codes of the Community Rule, the Damascus Document, and 4QMiscellaneous Rules (4Q265) (García Martínez, Tigchelaar and van der Woude, 1998: 433–34; Tigchelaar 2000: 285–92).

Further Reading: Dating, Physical Characteristics and Material Reconstruction of the Manuscripts

Alexander, P. S., 'The Redaction-History of Serekh ha-Yaḥad: a Proposal', *RevQ* 17 (1996), pp. 437–56.

Alexander, P. S. and G. Vermes, *Qumran Cave 4.XIX: Serekh ha-Yaḥad and Two Related Texts* (DJD 26; Oxford: Clarendon Press, 1998).

Bonani, G., M. Broshi, I. Carmi, S. Ivy, J. Strugnell, and W. Wölfli, 'Radiocarbon Dating of the Dead Sea Scrolls', *Atiqot* 20 (1991), pp. 27–32.

Cross, F. M., 'Paleographical Dates of the Manuscripts', in J. H. Charlesworth *et al.* (eds) *The Dead Sea Scrolls: Hebrew, Aramaic, and Greek Texts with English Translations*, vol. 1: *Rule of the Community and Related Documents* (Tübingen: J. C. B. Mohr [Paul Siebeck]; Louisville, KY: Westminster John Knox Press, 1994), p. 57.

Metso, S., *The Textual Development of the Qumran Community Rule* (STDJ, 21; Leiden: Brill, 1997), esp. pp. 13–68.

Milik, J. T., *The Books of Enoch: Aramaic Fragments of Qumrân Cave 4* (Oxford: Clarendon Press, 1976), esp. pp. 61–64 [on the dating of 4QS^e (*olim* 4QS^b)].

Qimron, E. and J. H. Charlesworth, with an Appendix by F. M. Cross, 'Cave IV Fragments (4Q255–264 = 4QS MSS A–J)', in Charlesworth *et al.* (eds), *The Dead Sea Scrolls. Hebrew, Aramaic, and Greek Texts with English Translations*, vol. 1: *Rule of the Community and Related Documents* (Tübingen: Mohr–Siebeck; Louisville, KY: Westminster John Knox, 1994), pp. 53–103.

Tov, E., *Scribal Practices and Approaches Reflected in the Texts Found in the Judean Desert* (STDJ, 54; Leiden: Brill, 2004).

Vermes, G., 'Preliminary Remarks on Unpublished Fragments of the Community Rule from Qumran Cave 4', *JJS* 42 (1991), pp. 250–55.

Chapter 2

GENRE AND CONTENTS

Fairly early in the study of the Qumran rule texts, in particular the Damascus Document and the Community Rule, the manuscripts were recognized to be composite documents, containing material from different sources originating from different periods of time. In terms of literary genre, these so-called rule texts are anything but homogeneous: in addition to the rules, we find, for example, theological expositions, liturgical and hymnic sections, even calendrical material.

Since 1QS is the best preserved of all the copies of the Community Rule, it is most convenient to use this manuscript when considering the contents and the detailed structure of the document. Methodologically, however, this is by no means unproblematic. Since there existed no standardized text, and since redaction involved not only combining larger units but also editing the smaller sections of the document, the structure of the text varies from one manuscript to another. The following discusses the structural units of 1QS with attention to the techniques used by the scribe of 1QS to mark divisions in the text. The most significant differences in the Cave 4 material are taken into consideration.

1QS I.1–15: Introduction

The main manuscript starts with an introduction that mentions several topics essential for life in the community. The centrality of the law of Moses is emphasized. The dualism which shaped the community's worldview is introduced, requiring strict separation between 'the sons of light' and 'the sons of darkness', that is, the community members and those outside. The community understands itself as the true keeper of the covenant, and its members strive for perfection in their ritual conduct. A command is given for obedience to the proper observance of cultic festivals according to the (solar) calendar used in the community. The members hand over their property for communal ownership. It has been suggested that the latter part of this introduction (I.11b–15) is directed to the candidates for admission to the community, while the beginning (I.1–11a) is addressed to the community's leaders (Knibb 1987: 79). No redactional seams can be detected, however, between the two parts; rather, the whole introduction seems to form a literary unity. This introduction at the beginning of 1QS can be compared with two other introductions in the same manuscript: 1QS V.1–7a and VIII.1–16a.

Very little of this introduction has remained among the fragments found in Cave 4. Two manuscripts have preserved some words from the first lines of the

document (4QS^a 1 = 1QS I.1–5; 4QS^c 1 I = 1QS I.2) and importantly, 4QS^a provides the full title of the document (ספר סרך היחד) which in 1QS is preserved
only partially. For the rest of the opening lines, the Cave 4 material provides no
readings that differ from 1QS.

1QS I.16–III.12: Liturgy for the Renewal of the Covenant

The opening of the liturgical section is more of a transition than a real heading
(Weise 1961: 64) and appears to be the work of the compiler. There are three subsections: 1QS I.16–II.18 describes the ceremony by which the members com-
mitted themselves to the covenant and new members were formally admitted,
II.19–25a presents the ritual for the annual covenant renewal by the community;
and II.25b–III.12 contains the curse upon those who are unwilling to commit themselves to the covenant or do so insincerely. After each part of the first subsection
the scribe has left a blank space as a paragraph division (I.20–21; II.11; II.18–
19). He also left a division between the priestly blessing and the Levitical curse
in II.4, and placed a paragraphos after II.18 to signal the beginning of the second
subsection of the text prescribing the annual covenant renewal.

The contents of the liturgical section are probably not original to this Rule but
possibly formed part of the ritual practices of the community prior to their inclusion in the Rule. To date there has been little inquiry as to whether all parts of this
section were already unified prior to their inclusion or the compiler of the Rule
joined disparate elements. There is broad agreement that the Hebrew Bible is the
basis of the liturgical patterns, the ideas, and sometimes even the wording of the
section (Leaney 1966: 105–107; Nitzan 1994: 129–135; for details, see Chapter 4,
below). The Cave 4 manuscripts show no major variants from 1QS in this section,
but 5Q11 has parallels with 1QS II.4–7 and 12–14(?) and displays some differences in the contents of the text of the liturgy.

1QS III.13–IV.26: Treatise on the Two Spirits

A unique theological section, introduced with למשכיל ('for the wise leader'), follows the liturgical section. It contains a sustained exposition of the community's
theological concepts found nowhere else in the Rule or the Qumran corpus. The
theme of this exposition is the fight between good and evil, with the underlying
presupposition of divine predestination. God has created two superhuman powers
who vie for influence over the good or evil that humans do. The Spirit of Truth
and the Spirit of Wickedness, also referred to as the Spirit of Light and the Spirit
of Darkness, seek to influence the actions and destiny of every human being.
From a cosmological perspective, every human is allotted to the dominion of one
or other of the two spirits. Somewhat inconsistently, from an anthropological
perspective every one is simultaneously swayed by both of the sprits. People
commit good or evil acts depending upon which of the spirits fighting in them
exercise greater dominion. When a righteous person commits an evil act, it is due
to the instigation of the Angel of Darkness, even though the Spirit of Light may
exercise dominant influence over the person's life in general.

The dualism in this passage is not absolute. The Prince of Darkness is not an independent and equal power alongside God; the text explicitly affirms that God created both the Spirit of Light and the Spirit of Darkness. God appointed them to influence the lives of mortals until a predetermined end, when the Spirit of Darkness will vanish and the Spirit of Truth will reign unchallenged. The community's dualistic beliefs may well have arisen from their eschatological conviction that they were living in the end time. The human struggle with the forces of evil would soon end: God would take control of human history, destroy all evil, and inaugurate an era where his dominion would not be challenged.

The scribe of 1QS began this theological section by leaving the end of the previous line blank and indenting a new line. He also left similar spaces at IV.1–2, 8–9, and 14–15, to mark the beginning of subsections. The manuscripts 4QS^a and possibly 4QS^h have preserved fragments relating to this section but they differ somewhat from 1QS, suggesting that this section too underwent redaction.

1QS V.1–VI.23 Rules for Community Life

The rules involving the community life are expounded in columns V and VI with introductory statements of the principles of the community's life, followed by a passage describing the oath to be taken by each member. Further regulations of community life continue, such as rules for separation from outsiders, for the meeting of the full members of the community (*ha-rabbîm* הרבים = 'the many'), and for accepting new members into the community. The manuscripts 4QS^b and 4QS^d provide a shorter and probably more original form of the text for these columns (Milik 1977: 78, Vermes 1991: 255, Metso 1997: 74–90; cf. Alexander 1996: 450–53). Additional parallels are provided by 4QS^g (1QS V.22–24; VI.3–5), 4QS^h (1QS V.26) and 4QS^i (1QS VI.1–3). In what follows, subsections of this large section are discussed separately.

1QS V.1–7a: Introduction

All manuscripts which have preserved the parallel to 1QS V.1 start the passage with a new column, signifying the beginning of a major section. In 4QS^d the text with the parallel of 1QS V.1 was also the beginning of the whole manuscript, suggesting that the 'Rule' as such originally started at this point, whereas the first four columns of the Cave 1 manuscript were later prefixed as introductory material. The heading in 1QS V.1 reads וזה הסרך לאנשי היחד ('This is the rule for the men of the community'), whereas 4QS^b and 4QS^d entitle the text מדרש למשכיל על אנשי התורה ('Teaching for the wise leader concerning the men of the Law'). The versions of the rules that follow in 4QS^{b,d} and 1QS differ greatly one from another, the former being shorter and probably more original. Both versions set out the general ideas and principles of the life of the community in the form of an introduction, but in the version of 1QS the section has been separated more clearly from the following legislative material. 1QS also adds a final sentence to the passage (1QS V.6b–7a) as well as a heading for the following section.

1QS V.7b–20a: Oath of the Members

This section speaks about the oath of those desiring to become members of the community. They are to bind themselves to the law of Moses (1QS V.7b–10a) and to separate from the men of injustice (1QS V.10b–20a). The text of the passage has undergone a particularly thorough redaction; the shorter version in 4QS[b,d] appears to have been the early form, while the version of 1QS develops it to more than twice the length of 4QS[b,d]. Whereas 4QS[b,d] has no title and commences with כול הבא לעצת היחד ('All who come to the council of the community'), 1QS prefixes a full title: ואלה תכון דרכיהם על כול החוקים האלה בהאספם ליחד ('These are their rules of conduct, according to all these statutes, when they are admitted to the community').

The syntax of the passage also suggests redaction. The scribe of 1QS left a space in the middle of line 13, and put a paragraphos mark in the margin. In 1QS, the third person plural referring to the men of injustice changes to the singular, although the theme of separation remains the same. After the citation of Exod. 23.7 in line 15b, plural forms are again used with reference of the wicked. It is difficult to see 1QS V.13b–15a as referring to a person joining the community, which is the topic of the main passage. These lines in 1QS seem rather to speak about one of the men of injustice, or about a person whose conversion is insincere. Some commentators on 1QS suspected that this passage was an interpolation even before the material from Cave 4 was available (Murphy-O'Connor 1969: 546–47; Knibb 1987: 110). The thought which originally flowed smoothly in 4QS[b,d] but is interrupted in 1QS at the end of line 13 continues at the end of line 15. The diction of the passage 1QS V.13b–15a is also very peculiar, for the particle כיא appears there five times. The problem of the number (whether singular or plural) does not come up at all in 4QS[b,d], for the long passage 1QS V.13b–15a is missing as well as the preceding passage in the plural form in V.11b–13a.

1QS V.20b–VI.1bα: Admission of New Members

The wording וכיא יבוא בברית לעשות ככול החוקים האלה ('When a man enters into the covenant to act according to all these statutes') introduces a passage dealing with the admission of new members and their annual examination. Except for a few glosses, the beginning of the section (1QS V.20b–25a) has very much the same contents in both editions 4QS[b,d] and 1QS, but the passage (i.e. 1QS V.25b–VI.1b) following the division space in the middle of line 1QS V.25 is largely missing in the version of 4QS[b,d]. A second and more detailed account of the procedure of the admission of new members is to be found further on in 1QS VI.13b–23.

1QS VI.1bβ–8a: Small Community Meetings in 'Their Dwelling Places'

A new heading באלה יתהלכו בכול מגוריהם כול הנמצא איש את רעהו ('In these [ways] shall they all walk in all their dwelling places, each with his neighbour' VI.1b–2a) begins a section which is different from the surrounding material, describing small-scale community meetings of ten members at the minimum who gather to eat, pray and take counsel. This is the only section in the Community Rule where the social setting is very unlikely to be the settlement at Qumran (for fuller discussion, see Chapter 4). The passage was joined to the composition by the way of inclusion: the preceding passage concludes with a reference to the *rabbîm* (1QS V.24b–VI.1a), and the end of this passage as well as the beginning of the following passage also make a reference to the *rabbîm* (VI.7; VI.8b). A fragmentary parallel to 1QS VI.1–7 is preserved in 4QS[d].

1QS VI.8b–13a: *Rule for the Session of the* Rabbim

A paragraph break and the heading הזה הסרך למושב הרבים ('This is the rule for the session of the *rabbîm*') mark the beginning of a rule for the session of the *rabbîm*, that is, of those included in the full membership of the community. The manuscripts 4QS[b,d] have preserved two small fragments belonging to this section. The form of the text seems to have been shorter there, although it cannot be reconstructed in its entirety.

The section highlights the strict hierarchy of the community in both the seating order and the order in which the members were allowed to address the *rabbîm*. At the head of the *rabbîm* is המבקר, 'the overseer'. Interestingly enough, the groups of the members of the community mentioned in this section are 'priests, elders and the rest of all the people', whereas in 1QS II.19–25b the groups are 'priests, Levites and all the people'. The terms elders (הזקנים) and Levites (הלויים) can hardly have been used synonymously, so it seems that two different traditions are represented here.

1QS VI.13b–23: *The Probationary Period of New Members*

The section describing the procedure for acceptance of a new member into the community begins not with a formal heading or paragraph division but with the topic announcement: וכול המתנדב מישראל להוסיף על עצת היחד ('Anyone who willingly offers himself from Israel to join the council of the community'). Selection of new members for admission was an important function performed by the *rabbîm*.

In order to become accepted as a full member of the community, the novice was tested through a lengthy probationary period in stages. The process began with preliminary acceptance by 'the officer in charge' (*ha-paqîd*) at the head of the *rabbîm*, and with investigation by the *rabbîm*. Upon approval the candidate began the first year of probation. He was not permitted at this stage to 'touch the purity of the *rabbîm*', which mainly involved participation in the common meal.

The next stage began with another examination, this time by the priests and the *rabbîm*. Upon approval the neophyte handed over his property to 'the overseer' (*ha-mebaqqer*) who listed it in the community records. A second year of probation followed, which, if successful, resulted in acceptance into full membership. The *rabbîm* alone are mentioned as the ones who make this final decision regarding permanent membership.

This section is similar to 1QS V.20b–VI.1a, but that passage describes the procedure in more general terms, and there is no mention of the officials entitled the *mebaqqer* (מבקר) and the *paqîd* (פקיד). The text of a small fragment from this section in 4QS[b] (par. 1QS VI.16–18) is shorter than 1QS, thus again pointing to a shorter and earlier version of the section. The sole fragment of 4QS^g from this section (1QS VI.22–25) is unfortunately too small to draw any conclusion regarding its relationship to 1QS.

1QS VI.24–VII.25: Penal Code

A section division, a paragraph sign in the margin, and the heading ואלה המשפטים אשר ישפטו בם במדרש יחד על פי הדברים ('These are the rules by which they shall judge at a community inquiry according to the cases') separate the new section consisting of the penal code from the preceding material, and a palaeo-Hebrew symbol at the end of column VII sets the section apart from the material in column VIII. The section has a distinct character, most of the judicial cases being introduced with the formula האיש אשר/ איש אשר / ואיש / אשר ואשר ('whoever…'). The penal code is very heterogeneous, the rules apparently collected somewhat haphazardly, but all of them reflect tensions in the community's life. The penal code may well have been compiled as the result of the court proceedings in the meetings of the *rabbîm*. The penalties vary from the punishment of ten days – the exact meaning of which is unclear, but it possibly involved reduction in the food ration – to permanent expulsion. The most severe transgressions included blasphemy, slandering the *rabbîm*, murmuring against the foundations of the community, and leaving the community after ten years of membership. The literary genre of this section is that of casuistic law, as, for example, paralleled in the Book of the Covenant (Exod. 20.22–23.33).

Two other manuscripts, 4QS^e and 4QS^g, have preserved material parallel to this section. From the title (see above) 4QS^g lacks the words בם במדרש יחד, but 4QS^{e,g} display no other major differences from 1QS except for some changes in the length of punishments. For example, the order of the offenses is the same, which is quite surprising, considering the heterogeneous character of the offenses. The editorial corrections of the second scribe at the end of column 1QS VII largely follow the text of 4QS^e (no parallel has been preserved for the beginning of the column in 4QS^g or 4QS^e).

1QS VIII.1–IX.26a: 'Manifesto' or Segments of Early Rules

The character of columns 1QS VIII–IX has been highly debated among scholars. Some commentators, following E. F. Sutcliffe (1959: 134–38) and A. R. C. Leaney (1966: 112, 115, 211), suppose that this section forms the core of the document and refers to the time of the founding of the community, representing a kind of 'Manifesto' or 'programme of the community' (Murphy-O'Connor 1969: 529). H. Stegemann, on the other hand, argues that the whole of columns VIII and IX consists of secondary additions (1998: 111–12).

Particularly difficult to interpret has been the material in 1QS VIII.1–IX.11 preceding the sections addressed to the wise leader (1QS IX.12–26). Introductory formulas outline the structure of this part of the text. The formula בהיות אלה בישראל ('When these exist in Israel') appears three times, in 1QS VIII.4b,12b

and IX.3. The section VIII.10b–12a starts with the formula בהכין אלה ביסוד
היחד ('When these have been established in the fundamental principles of the
community') and the section VIII.20–IX.2 with the formula ואלה המשפטים אשר
ילכו בם ('These are the rules by which they shall walk'). The section VIII.16b–
19 has no introductory formula, but as a penal code it clearly differs from the
preceding material. This penal code may be compared with the longer penal code
in column VI. Two sections addressed to the 'wise leader' (*maskîl*; 1QS IX.12
and 21) form the latter part of column IX. They describe the qualities and responsibilities of the community's spiritual leader.

The language of the columns is highly idealized, painting a picture of an ethi-
cally superior way of life and piety. The community is described as the true
temple, in which prayer has replaced the sacrificial offerings; the community's
condemnation of the Jerusalem temple is implicitly present in the text. The motivation for withdrawal into the desert is provided by a quotation from the book of
Isaiah: 'In the wilderness prepare the way of the Lord' (Isa. 40.3), which is identified with the study of the law (VIII.12–16). The section may well mirror the
attitudes of the pious Jews who had been offended by the Hasmonean rulers' way
of managing the affairs of the Jewish community. The group's withdrawal into
the desert took place presumably sometime between 150 and 100 BCE, as archaeological evidence indicates that this was the time when Essene habitation in
Khirbet Qumran first started (de Vaux 1973; Magness 2002).

The evidence of manuscript 4QS[e] sheds new light on the problem. In 4QS[e] the
passage parallel to 1QS VIII.15b–IX.11 is not present. An argument can be made
that the passage is a secondary insertion in 1QS consisting of three smaller interpolations (Metso 1993: 304–305). Two of them (1QS VIII.16b–19 and VIII.20–
IX.2) provide a code of discipline, and the third one (IX.3–11) is a duplicate
based on 1QS VIII.1–15a. In the light of 4QS[e] it seems that the section parallel to
1QS VIII.1–15a formed an introductory passage for the following sections
addressed to the wise leader. Although these regulations for the wise leader may
be of early origin, in light of 4QS[e] it might be more appropriate to speak simply
of an introduction rather than of a manifesto. This introduction is comparable
with two other introductions in 1QS, namely with those at the beginning of
column I and of column V.

Moreover, a comparison between manuscripts 4QS[d] and 4QS[e] indicates that
the original form of the introduction of column VIII consisted of 1QS VIII.1–
13a+15a, and did not include the citation of Isa. 40.3 found in 1QS VIII.13b–14.
That passage was inserted later, presumably in order to provide a scriptural basis
for the community's withdrawal into the desert. The addition was most likely
made by the same redactor who was responsible for the work of editing in columns 1QS V–VII (cf. 4QS[b,d]). It is interesting to note that all four Gospels cite
this same quotation but apply it to John the Baptist preaching in the desert to
prepare the way for Jesus (Mt. 3.3; Mk 1.3; Lk. 3.4-6; Jn 1.23).

The section 1QS IX.12–26a addressed to the wise leader (למשכיל) is divided
into two parts by a paragraph division and a new heading (ואלה תכוני הדרך
למשכיל 'These are the rules of conduct for the wise leader'; IX.21), which is

very similar to the one in 1QS IX.12. Since the passages IX.12–21aα and IX.21aβ–26a are stylistically coherent, it is very difficult to assume any redactional joins between them. Other sections addressed to the wise leader in the Community Rule are the introduction in 1QS I.1–15, the treatise on the two spirits 1QS III.13–IV.26 and the parallel to 1QS V in manuscripts 4QS^{b,d}. It cannot, however, be assumed that there is a common source behind the material of these sections.

1QS IX.26b–XI.22: Final Psalm

The document concludes with a hymn, which is introduced by a calendrical section listing the community's times of prayer. The final psalm in 1QS with its calendrical section at the beginning had an independent existence before its insertion in the composition. This can be demonstrated with the aid of the material reconstruction of the manuscript 4QS^e, which concluded with a different calendrical text 4QOtot. The manuscript 4QS^e shows, in addition, that the calendar of prayer times in 1QS IX.26b–X.8a did not originally belong with the sections addressed to the wise leader (1QS IX.12–26a), but was introduced into the composition together with the psalm. The first sentence at the beginning of the calendrical section (1QS IX.26b–X.1a) functions as a link, and it was presumably created by the compiler. The psalm provides an intimate portrait of Essene piety, which is both humble and celebratory, conscious of profound human sinfulness, but conscious also of the richness of divine mercy and their special chosenness as recipients of heavenly secrets.

Further Reading: Commentaries and General Introductions with Discussions on the Serekh

Elledge, C. D., *The Bible and the Dead Sea Scrolls* (Archaeology and Biblical Studies, 14; Atlanta: Society of Biblical Literature, 2005).

Gracía Martínez, F. and J. Trebolle Barrera, *The People of the Dead Sea Scrolls: Their Writings, Beliefs and Practices* (trans. W. G. E. Watson; Leiden: Brill, 1993).

Knibb, M. A., *The Qumran Community* (Cambridge Commentaries on Writings of the Jewish and Christian World 200 BC to AD 200, 2; Cambridge: Cambridge University Press, 1987).

Leaney, A. R. C., *The Rule of Qumran and Its Meaning: Introduction, Translation and Commentary* (London: SCM Press, 1966).

Nickelsburg, G. A., *Jewish Literature between the Bible and the Mishnah* (Minneapolis: Fortress Press, 2nd edn, 2005).

VanderKam, J., *The Dead Sea Scrolls Today* (Grand Rapids: Eerdmans, 1994).

VanderKam, J. and P. Flint, *The Meaning of the Dead Sea Scrolls* (San Francisco: HarperSanFrancisco, 2002).

Wernberg-Møller, P., *The Manual of Discipline Translated and Annotated with an Introduction* (STDJ, 1; Leiden: Brill, 1957).

Chapter 3

PHASES OF TEXTUAL GROWTH

From the very beginning of research on the Community Rule the document has been acknowledged as a collection from various sources (e.g., del Medico 1951: 27–30; Dupont-Sommer 1953: 90; Wernberg-Møller 1957: 56 n. 49). Based on the internal evidence of 1QS, several studies focusing on the redaction history of the Community Rule appeared between the 1950s and the 1980s. Since exhaustive summaries regarding this early stage of research are available elsewhere (e.g., Bardtke 1974: 257–91; Delcor 1979: 851–57; Murphy-O'Connor 1986: 128–29), I will focus here only on those theories which have contributed most to the redaction-critical study of 1QS. The material of Cave 4 did not become widely accessible until the 1990s, and its analysis is still in an early stage, but the results that have been achieved already offer promise of a lively discussion in the near future. In what follows, I shall first outline the main lines of discussion prior to the publication of the Cave 4 manuscripts, and then summarize the approaches taken to the Cave 4 material.

Composition of 1QS

The idea that became a central building block for many subsequent theories regarding the redaction of the Community Rule was presented by E. F. Sutcliffe in 1959 (pp. 134–38). He proposed that columns VIII–IX of 1QS represent the earliest material of the document, reflecting the stage immediately prior to the founding of the community; the formula בהיות אלה בישראל 'When these exist in Israel' that occurs three times (VIII.4,12; IX.3) he saw as a reference to the community soon to be established. Ten years later, J. Murphy-O'Connor (1969: 528–49; 1986: 129) named this part of the text a 'Manifesto' of the community (VIII.1–16; IX.3–X.8), and argued that there was a three-stage development from this nucleus. In the first stage of redaction, 'penal legislation for a small community' (VIII.16–IX.2) was attached to the Manifesto. Secondly, 'the community redefined itself (V.1–13) and enacted more elaborate legislation (V.15–VII.25)'. In the final stage, 'material from various sources was combined to form an exhortation to authentic observance (I.1–IV.26; X.9–XI.22)'. As seen by Murphy-O'Connor, these four redactional stages corresponded to the four archaeological phases of Khirbet Qumran as outlined by R. de Vaux (1973).

Murphy-O'Connor's theory was developed and modified in the 1970s and 1980s in publications by various scholars. J. Pouilly (1976) essentially followed

Murphy-O'Connor's theory in presuming four layers of text in 1QS, but he assigned VIII.10–12 not to the Manifesto, but to the first stage of redaction, and V.13–VI.8 not to the second stage but the final stage. Puech (1979b; 1993: 421–22) suggested that the text evolved in three stages instead of four, the first one being constituted by parts of columns VIII–IX (le noyau de fondation), the second by columns V–VII (motivations d'entrée dans la communauté et le code penitentiel) with the exception of some additions, and the third stage by columns I–IV (composition liturgique et doctrinale) and IX–XI (considérations pour l'instructeur et hymnes). P. Arata Mantovani (1983: 69–91) also presupposed three stages in the development of the text, but he divided them somewhat differently: VIII.1–IX.26 (tradizione A), V.1–13a,15b–VII.25 (tradizione B), I–IV; V.13b–15a; X, 4b, 6a.9–XI.22 (tradizione C). C. Dohmen (1982: 81–96), on the other hand, found three different stages of development in columns VIII–IX alone: (1) VIII.1–7a+12b–15a+IX.16b–21a (das Manifest); (2) VIII.7b–12a/IX.12–16a+IX.21b–26 (die Erweiterung des Manifestes); and (3) IX.3–11+VIII.15b–19/VIII.20–IX.2 (die 'erste Regel' und ihre Erweiterung).

A different approach was taken by D. Dimant (1984: 501–502), who rejected the idea that textual stages would reflect the different life-situations in the community. In her view, the redactional motivation was 'literary-ideological' instead. She detected 'apparent doublets' within the composition and proposed that the redactor(s) followed a chiastic pattern in arranging the material. Another approach also fundamentally differing from that of Murphy-O'Connor was presented by H. Stegemann (1998:107–16), who saw 1QS not as an independent document, but as a part of a collection consisting of four different community rules (Gemeindeordnungen): (1) 1QS I.1–III.12 (die Gemeinschaftsordnung), (2) 1QS V.1–XI.22 (die Disziplinarordnung), (3) 1QSa (die älteste Gemeindeordnung der Essener), and (4) 1QSb (die Segensordnung). In Stegemann's view, 1QS III.13–IV.26, which includes the treatise on the two spirits, formed an appendix to 1QS I.1–III.12 (Gemeinschaftsordnung). 'Die Disziplinarordnung', (V.1–XI.22) he thinks, is a collection of organizational regulations developed successively in the first decades of the Essenes' *yaḥad*. Stegemann refers to the earlier versions of the text found in Cave 4 and maintains that the form of the text represented by 1QS V.1–XI.22 represents the latest phase of the development of this rule.

In addition, it is important to consider studies focusing on the features of 1QS VII–VIII that display the work of two different scribes. The foundational, and to date the most exhaustive, analyses distinguishing the typical features of the two hands (A and B) were made by M. Martin (1958: 439–42) and P. Guilbert (1958). Martin argued that scribe B had used a revisor exemplar while revising the text, while Guilbert suggested that most of the additions and corrections made by scribe B were made without the aid of another written manuscript. According to Guilbert, scribe B had interpreted the text in a rather personal way. The work of the two scribes has been further analyzed by É. Puech (1979a). As was not the case with Martin and Guilbert, Puech was able to make use of the list of 4QS variants which had meanwhile been published by Milik (1960). Puech came to a conclusion very similar to that of Martin: at least some of the corrections in column

VII were based on another manuscript, which, in Puech's view, was perhaps 4QS^e. Although he admits that some of the additions made by B are not included in 4QS^e, he argues that they may have been present in some other manuscript more contemporary with 1QS.

Contribution of the Cave 4 Material

The evidence of the Cave 4 copies both illuminates and complicates the textual history. J. Milik in 1977 suggested that 4QS^{b,d} with a shorter text represent an earlier form of the document than 1QS. G. Vermes agreed in 1991, paying special attention to a variant referring to the authority of the community. The words 'according to the *rabbim*' in 4QS^{b,d} were replaced by a longer formulation in 1QS V.2–3: 'according to the sons of Zadok, the priests who keep the covenant, and to the multitude of the men of the community who hold fast to the covenant; on their word the decision shall be taken on any matter having to do with the law, with wealth, or with justice.' Whereas Vermes speaks of two different traditions, C. Hempel (1996: 253–69) has developed the thought further, speaking of a Zadokite recension, the marks of which can also be seen in the text of the Rule of the Congregation (1QSa), a different composition copied on the same scroll with 1QS. R. Kugler (1996) discusses another variant concerning בני הצדק/בני הצדוק in 1QS IX.14 / 4QS^e III.10, arguing that the form in 1QS typifies a later recension which indicates that the Zadokite priests had not always had a prominent role in the community but gained that position only at a later stage. In his view the Zadokites, however, remained obedient to the superior *maskîl*.

P. Alexander (1996: 437–56) begins from the principle that the order in which the manuscripts were copied holds the key to the order in which the different recensions were created. 1QS, which is generally dated to about 100–75 BCE, contains a longer version. The manuscripts 4QS^b and 4QS^d, which were copied a half century later, in the last third of the last century BCE, have preserved a shorter version of the document than 1QS. Alexander, in contrast to Milik and Vermes, considers 4QS^{b,d} the result of intentional omissions from the longer document. His explanation of the variant in 1QS V.2–3 versus 4QS^{b,d} (above) is that 1QS reflects an early stage in the history of the community when the Zadokites held a leading position, whereas 4QS^{b,d} belong to a later stage when their position had weakened. The manuscript 4QS^e lacks the large section VIII.15–IX.11 in 1QS. Alexander thinks that this was an intentional omission, after the redactor observed contradictions and repetitions in that section. As to the relationship between 4QS^{b,d} and 4QS^e, Alexander sees 4QS^e as the latest redactional stage. Thus, his suggestion of the order of the MSS is: 1QS (oldest), 4QS$^{(b),d}$, 4QS^e (youngest).

The possibility of abbreviation has also been brought up by J. Charlesworth and B. A. Strawn who, referring to Vermes' observation that 4QS^d never included a text parallel to 1QS I–IV, ask: 'Is it not conceivable that a larger block of the Rule of the Community was excerpted in MS D for some reason?', and tentatively respond: 'Only more research can tell, but in our opinion the answer is yes' (1996: 415). Charlesworth and Strawn point out, however, that 'we must endeavor to guard against assuming that a late paleographical date implies a later and dependent version ... we may have multiple versions with multiple textual and tradition histories, both prior to and even after the compilation of 1QS' (1996: 414). In the conclusion of their article this cautious approach does not seem operative, for they write: 'We have shown that Qumran compositions were sometimes abbreviated for private use and the needs of a leader, probably the Maskil' (1996: 432). P. Garnet in his analysis of 4QS^{b,d} reckons with 1QS and 4QS^{b,d} sharing a common ancestor and 4QS^{b,d} depending on 'a partially epitomized text of the Community Rule' (1997: 75). Garnet writes that 'there are instances where the B/D text clearly preserves older readings than 1QS (e.g. the parallels to 1QS 7.12 and 8.5), but the evidence points to the probability that the common ancestor was more like 1QS than B/D' (1997: 75–76).

S. Metso (1997), in a literary- and redaction-critical analysis of the Cave 4 manuscripts (4QS^{a-j}), presents a comprehensive treatment of the *Serekh* variants. She sees 1QS as a relatively late stage in the development of the document and considers the forms transmitted by 4QS^e, and 4QS^{b,d}, as forerunners of that in 1QS. First, with regard to 4QS^{b,d}, the main characteristics of the redaction that can be detected by comparing 4QS^{b,d} and 1QS were the need to provide scriptural legitimization for the rules of the community and to strengthen the group's self-understanding as the true keeper of the covenant and the law. Secondly, the redaction observed by comparing 4QS^e and 1QS indicates that 1QS aimed at bringing the text up to date. Thus, 4QS^e and 4QS^{b,d} represent two lines of tradition which derive from an earlier version, a version which (1) as witnessed by 4QS^d, did not include the material parallel to 1QS I–IV; (2) as witnessed by 4QS^d, commenced with the text parallel to 1QS V and was addressed to the *maskil*; (3) as witnessed by 4QS^{b,d}, did not yet have the scriptural quotations or the additions aimed at strengthening the community's self-understanding; (4) as witnessed by 4QS^e, did not yet include the section parallel to 1QS VIII.15–IX.11; and (5) as witnessed by 4QS^e, lacked the final psalm found in 1QS X–XI but possibly included (as does 4QS^e) the calendrical text Otot. The redaction as found in 1QS is a combination of both lines of tradition as in 4QS^e and 4QS^{b,d}, and thus includes both the final psalm and the scriptural quotations and community-oriented additions. The latest stage of redaction is to be seen in the revisions and additions made even later by the scribal corrector in 1QS VII–VIII. Thus the plurality of textual forms indicates that the community had continued copying older versions even when newer, expanded versions were available. In this she points to the parallel of the biblical manuscripts, most clearly for Exodus and Jeremiah, where the same phenomenon is documented (Metso 2000b: 381–82).

The above-mentioned theories have been compared and discussed by M. Bockmuehl (1998), who considers the priority of 4QS^{b,d} 'a sound hypothesis' and observes that 'the effect of the redactional changes in 1QS is not so much to innovate as to reinforce, and to make more explicit certain tendencies of community doctrine and discipline that are already present in the earlier text forms'. In his view, the redaction in 1QS 'suggests a tightening religious practice in which atonement and forgiveness were increasingly limited to the sect itself and religious authority is concentrated in the hands of Zadokite priests' (1998: 557). Following Hempel's hypothesis (see above), Bockmuehl sees a pro-Zadokite emphasis also in 1QSa and 1QSb which were copied in the same scroll with 1QS. Another evaluation of the current state of research is available in an article by M. Knibb (2000) in the *Encyclopaedia of the Dead Sea Scrolls*. In his view, 'Alexander's stress on the importance of paleography has to be taken seriously. On the other hand, the view put forward by Metso better takes account of the indications within 1QRule of the Community itself that the text is composite, and that it acquired its present form by a process of evolution' (2000: 796).

Further Reading on the Textual History of the Serekh

Alexander, P. S., 'The Redaction History of Serekh Ha-Yaḥad: A Proposal', *RevQ* 17 (1996), pp. 437–56.

Bockmuehl, M., 'Redaction and Ideology in the Rule of the Community (1QS/4QS)', *RevQ* 18 (1998), pp. 541–60.

Charlesworth, J., and B. A. Strawn, 'Reflections on Text of Serekh ha-Yaḥad Found in Cave 4', *RevQ* 17 (1996), pp. 403–35.

Davies, P. R., 'Redaction and Sectarianism in the Qumran Scrolls', in F. García Martínez, A. Holhorst and C. J. Labuschagne (eds), *The Scriptures and the Scrolls: Studies in Honour of A.S. van der Woude on the Occasion of his 65th Birthday* (VTSup, 49; Leiden: Brill, 1992), pp. 152–63.

Dimant, D., 'Qumran Sectarian Literature', in M. E. Stone (ed.), *Jewish Writings of the Second Temple Period* (CRINT, 2.2; Assen: Van Gorcum; Philadelphia: Fortress Press, 1984), pp. 483–550.

Garnet, P., 'Cave 4 MS Parallels to 1QS 5.1–7: Towards a *Serek* Text History', *JSP* 15 (1997), pp. 67–78.

Guilbert, P., 'Deux écritures dans les colonnes VII et VIII de la Règle de la Communauté', *RevQ* 1 (1958), pp. 199–212.

—'Le plan de la Régle de la Communauté', *RevQ* 3 (1959), pp. 323–44.

Hempel, C., 'Comments on the Translation of 4QS[d] I,1', *JJS* 44 (1993), pp. 127–28.

Martin, M., *The Scribal Character of the Dead Sea Scrolls, I–II* (Louvain: Publications universitaires, 1958).

Metso, S., *The Textual Development of the Qumran Community Rule* (STDJ, 21; Leiden: Brill, 1997).

—'The Textual Traditions of the Qumran Community Rule', in M. J. Bernstein, F. García Martínez, and J. Kampen (eds), *Legal Texts and Legal Issues: Proceedings of the Second Meeting of the International Organization for Qumran Studies, Cambridge 1995* (Leiden: Brill, 1997), pp. 141–47.

—'The Redaction of the Community Rule', in L. H. Schiffman, E. Tov, and J. C. VanderKam (eds), *Proceedings of the International Congress 'The Dead Sea Scrolls: Fifty Years After Their Discovery'* (Jerusalem: Israel Exploration Society/Shrine of the Book Museum, Israel , 2000), pp. 377–84.

Milik, J.T., 'Milkî-ṣedeq et Milkî-resa' dans les anciens écrits juifs et chrétiens', *JJS* 23 (1972), pp. 95–144.

Murphy-O'Connor, J., 'La genèse littéraire de la Règle de la Communauté', *RB* 76 (1969), pp. 528–49.

Pouilly, J., *La Règle de la Communauté: Son evolution littéraire* (Cahiers de la Revue Biblique, 17; Paris: Gabalda, 1976).

Stegemann, H., *The Library of Qumran: On the Essenes, Qumran, John the Baptist, and Jesus* (orig. *Die Essener, Qumran, Johannes der Täufer und Jesus: Ein Sachbuch* [Freiburg: Herder, 1993]; Grand Rapids: Eerdmans; Leiden: Brill, 1998).

Vermes, G., 'Preliminary Remarks on Unpublished Fragments of the Community Rule from Qumran Cave 4', *JJS 42* (1991), pp. 250–55.

Chapter 4

COMMENTARY ON KEY PASSAGES

General Principles of Community Life

The general ethos of the life of the Qumran community is perhaps best illustrated by the three introductory passages at the beginning of columns I, V, and VIII of 1QS, all of which are quite similar in the themes they emphasize. Comparison between the different copies of S, however, indicates that these passages were brought into the composition at different stages of redaction. In 4QS^b, the introduction parallel to 1QS V.1–7 is the beginning of the whole manuscript, for there was no parallel to 1QS I–IV included in this manuscript. Moreover, the introduction in 4QS^b IX.1–6 // 4QS^d I.1–5 seems to have been originally written for only the legislative material parallel to 1QS V–VII rather than for the entire content of V–IX. The redaction, which can be seen in 1QS V.1–7, was probably carried out after the material of columns 1QS V–VII and VIII–IX were linked together; the purpose of the revision may have been to make the introduction of 1QS V.1–7 cover the material of columns 1QS VIII–IX, too, and thus combine columns V–VII and VIII–IX more closely. The introduction of 1QS I.1–15 was probably intended to tie the whole of the composition of S together, not simply the liturgical and theological material of columns 1QS I–IV, for this introduction deals with themes that pertain to the whole document rather than only to those discussed in columns I–IV.

The Community Rule in many respects overlaps with the information provided by ancient historians Philo, Pliny and especially Josephus on the Essenes. Regarding the parallels with Josephus, T. Beall has observed that 'many of the parallels mentioned above are rather general qualities that might fit many groups (mutual affection, self-control, despising riches, etc.), and thus are not particularly helpful in deciding whether the Qumran community was Essene or not. But the sheer number of parallels is striking, and puts the burden of proof upon those who would insist that the Qumran community was *not* Essene' (1988: 125). The central themes of the introductory passages are discussed in what follows.

Adherence to and Study of the Law of Moses

All of the introductory passages stress the community's commitment to seek God's will in accordance with the Torah (cf. 1QS I.1–3; 1QS V.1; 4QS^b IX.1 // 4QS^d I.1; 1QS VIII.1–2). Josephus, too, testifies that the Essenes 'display an extraordinary interest in the writings of the ancients' (*War* II.136; trans. Thackeray).

The sheer volume of writings discovered in the remains of the Essene library at Qumran, including numerous biblical manucripts, commentaries and other exegetical works, provides strong evidence of diligent study and copying of Scriptures. According to 1QS VI.6–8 the study of the Torah was to be continually maintained in the community, even to be carried out during one third of each night. Interpretation of holy writings was a source for new revelation and divine guidance for the community during the era of Belial in which the community thought it was living.

The Ethical Obligation of the Community

The virtues of truth, righteousness, justice, humility, kindly love and circumspection were held in high regard in the community, and were expected of the members in their mutual conduct (1QS I.5–6, V.3–4; 4QS^b IX.3–4 // 4QS^d I.3, VIII.2). The wording in 1QS I.5–6 'they shall practise truth, righteousness, and justice' appears to be based on *T. Ben.* 10.3, but 1QS V.3–4 and VIII.2 include a phrase from Mic. 6.8 as well: 'justice, kindly love and circumspection' (Knibb 1987: 80, 106, 130). According to Josephus, the Essenes show 'a greater attachment to each other than do the other sects', and a person aspiring to join the community made a commitment to 'practice piety towards the Deity, [and] observe justice towards men' (*War* II. 119, 139).

Separation from Outsiders

Those outside community were considered as belonging to the realm of darkness and, therefore, strict separation from them was required. They were 'sons of darkness' (1QS I.10) and 'men of injustice' (1QS V.2; VIII.13), guilty and deserving of God's vengeance (I.10–11). This corresponds to the community's dualistic worldview, outlined in detail in the treatise on the two spirits (1QS III.13–IV.26). Separation was necessary also in order to guard the ritual purity of the community. As Knibb says: 'the demand for separation was no doubt based on a desire to avoid contamination through contact with outsiders, who were regarded as unclean; but in making this demand the community was merely appropriating to itself the priestly and levitical ideals of the Old Testament' (1987: 109).

Bearers of Expiation

The community saw itself as participating in the judgement of the wicked and bringing of atonement. This theme is particularly prominent in the introduction of 1QS VIII: 'They shall be accepted to make expiation for the land and to determine the judgment of wickedness; and there shall be no more injustice' (1QS VIII.10). The theme of atonement also occurs in 1QS V.6–7, but there it is a result of redaction, for in 4QS^b IX.5 // 4QS^d I.4 the theme is absent. There is no mention of atonement in the introduction of 1QS I, but the members are invited to 'hate all the sons of darkness, each according to his guilt in the vengeance of God' (1QS I.10–11). One of the obligations of the Essenes listed by Josephus is to 'for ever hate the unjust and fight the battle of the just' (*War* II.139).

Keeping the Covenant
The community's self-understanding as the true keeper of the covenant is emphasized in each of the introductions. According to 1QS VIII.10, the very purpose of
the community's existence was to 'establish the covenant according to the eternal
statutes'. According to 1QS I.7, admitting new members into the community was
identified with bringing 'into the covenant of love those who willingly offer
themselves to observe the statutes of God' (1QS I.7). This statement appears to
anticipate the yearly ceremony of the covenant renewal, the liturgy of which follows the introduction. In this ceremony new members were formally admitted into
the community. In 1QS V.2–3, the question of the authority in the community is
linked with the issue of keeping the covenant: those joining the community are
said to be answerable to the priests called the 'sons of Zadok' and to 'the men of
the community', whose special responsibility was to guard the covenant. Interestingly, in the version of 4QS[b,d] we find a simple reference to the *rabbîm* ('the
many') instead of the more specific statement in 1QS.

Calendar
1QS I.13–15 makes the point that 'the appointed times' and 'feasts' should be
observed as commanded by God, not anticipating them or falling behind. This is
a clear reference to the solar calendar of the Essenes, different from the lunar
calendar observed by the community in Jerusalem. The issue of calendar is more
thoroughly dealt with in 1QS X.1–8; the fact that the theme is mentioned at the
beginning of the document seems to indicate that the introduction of 1QS I.1–15
was intended for the whole of the composition, not for columns 1QS I–IV only.
The introduction of 1QS VIII also makes a brief mention of the calendar: the
members of the community were expected to conduct themselves according to
'the rule of the time' (1QS VIII.4).

Common Property
For the topic of the life in the community, the mention of the community members' wealth in 1QS I.13 is of interest. The passage states that those offering themselves for membership were expected to bring 'all their knowledge, their abilities,
and their wealth into the community'. That the community described in 1QS held
its property in common is clear from VI.18–21: submitting one's property to the
community formed one element in the lengthy process of admission. Again, the
very fact that an issue which is properly dealt with only in the latter half of the
document is mentioned at the beginning of the document, indicates that whoever
composed the introduction of 1QS I, intended it for the whole composition.
Josephus was well aware of the sharing of property among the Essenes, for he
writes about them that 'they despise riches' (*War* II.122), and that 'there is no
buying or selling among themselves, but each gives what he has to any in need
and receives from him in exchange something useful to himself; they are, moreover, freely permitted to take anything from any of their brothers without making
any return' (*War* II.127).

The Covenant Ceremony

The concept of covenant, a pact between God and Israel, was central for the theology and identity of the *yaḥad* community. While affirming the eternal validity of the covenant, the community considered itself as the only true keeper of the covenant, thus effectively excluding the rest of Israel. Joining the community was identified with entering the covenant. Moreover, it was in the context of a covenant ceremony (1QS I.16–III.12) that the formal admission of new members took place and the membership of already existing members was reaffirmed.

The importance of the covenant ceremony is attested by its position at the beginning of the document immediately after the introduction that already states as one of the main goals: 'they shall admit into the covenant of love all those who willingly offer themselves to observe the statutes of God' (1QS I.7). The ceremony served the important tasks of strengthening the identity of the members as those belonging to 'the lot of God', as opposed to the 'lot of Belial', and of warning them against backsliding 'through any fear or terror or trial which takes place during the reign of Belial' (1QS I.17).

Parts of the covenant liturgy have been preserved in a number of the manuscripts. Although the copy from Cave 1 is the only one to have fully preserved the text of the covenant liturgy, four copies from Cave 4 (4QS[a-c, h]) have preserved fragmentary parallels to the material in 1QS I.16–III.12. One of the Cave 4 manuscripts (4QS[d]), however, never included the covenant ceremony, for it began only with the rules and regulations that start at 1QS V.1, excluding the theological and liturgical sections of 1QS I–IV. The case of 4QS[e] is less certain, but it too may not have included the material of 1QS I–IV.

The text of 1QS I.16–III.12 can be divided into three parts: the liturgy for the ceremony of entry of new members is described in 1QS I.16–II.18, and it is followed by a less detailed description of the annual renewal of the covenant by current members in II.19–25a. It is unlikely that these two sections would indicate two separate ceremonies. Rather, it seems that new members were formally admitted during the annual renewal of the covenant. The third part in II.25b–III.12 does not so much describe a ceremony as discuss the fate of those who refuse to enter the covenant or do so with an impure heart; it is questionable whether the section was ever recited as a part of the ceremony. On the whole, it is unclear how accurately the text in 1QS corresponded to the actual course of the liturgy. D. Falk, for example, characterizes 1QS I.18–II.18 as 'an incomplete description, seemingly for rhetorical purposes rather than instructions for performance' (Falk 1998: 219).

The ceremony described in 1QS I.16–II.18 consists of four parts. In the first part, the priests and Levites bless 'the God of Salvation' and his faithful deeds, to which the people respond 'Amen, amen' (I.18b–20). In the second part, the priests recount God's righteous acts towards Israel, and then the Levites recount the iniquities of the children of Israel, after which all entering the covenant confess their sins (I.21–II.1a). In the third part, the priests bless 'the men of God's lot', the Levites curse 'the men of Belial's lot', and those entering the covenant respond 'Amen, amen' (II.1b–10). In the final part, the priests and Levites together curse those who might have entered into the covenant insincerely. Those entering the covenant respond again 'Amen, amen' (II.11–18).

The various components of this liturgy are based on biblical precedents, as B. Nitzan and others have observed: 'these recitations reflect the conventional formula used in the Bible for ceremonies of renewal of the covenant following its violation (compare 1 Sam. 12.6-25; Ezra 9.6-10; Neh. 9.10, 30); while the lit-urgical formula of participation by priests, Levites and the community, and the framework of antiphonal recitations and response, are taken from the ceremony at Mt. Gerizim and Mt. Ebal described in Deuteronomy 27' (Nitzan 1994: 129–30). The confession of sins in 1QS I.24–26 may be compared with similar confessions in Ps. 106.6; 1 Kgs 8.47; Jer. 3.25; Dan. 9.5 (Weise 1961: 79–80). The blessing in II.2b–4 is clearly based on the priestly blessing in Num. 6.24-26. The curse in II.4b–10 has its precedent in Deut. 27.14-26. Utilizing biblical examples, the *yaḥad* community created a liturgical combination that in its specific form remains unique in Second Temple literature (Nitzan 1994: 130; Falk 1998: 222).

Deuteronomy 31.9-13 stipulates that the renewal of the covenant was to take place every seven years at the Feast of Sukkoth. In the *yaḥad*, however, the renewal was observed annually, presumably during the Feast of Shabu'ot, for 4QD^a frg. 11 line 17 // 4QD^e frg. 7 ii.11–12 speak about an annual gathering of people in the third month. The book of Jubilees supports the Feast of Shabu'ot as the time for the renewal ceremony, insofar as it prescribes that the fifteenth day of the third month is the date for celebrating Shabu'ot and the renewal of the covenant (*Jub.* 6.17-19).

Weise (1961: 79 n. 2, 85, 89 n. 2) suggested that the lengthy psalm (IX.26–XI.22) which concludes 1QS should be associated with the covenant ceremony in 1QS I–III, and possibly formed part of the covenant liturgy (1961: 79 n. 2, 85, 89 n. 2). There are indeed extensive verbal similarities between the passages (see table in Falk 1998: 111). It is peculiar however, that if the hymn were really a part of the covenant-renewal ceremony, it was not placed together with other passages constituting the ceremony. Moreover, 4QS^d includes the final psalm, but not the material of 1QS I–IV which contains the ceremony. It is more likely, as H.-W. Kuhn (1966: 31–32) has suggested that elements of the covenant ceremony were taken over into the practice of daily prayer. Falk agrees with Kuhn, pointing out that 'it could be that the parallels are purely literary and that the concluding hymn reflects a conscious effort to recall the covenant ceremony for rhetorical effect' (Falk 1998: 111).

Several texts found at Qumran have preserved material pertaining to the cove-nant ceremony: The fragmentary 5Q13, entitled simply as 'Rule', has preserved two brief citations from 1QS III.4–5 and 1QS II.19 in fragment 4, but it is likely that a fuller description of a ceremony similar to the one in the Community Rule was included the manuscript. The Damascus Document, though not including a description of the covenant-renewal ceremony, at the end of the admonition includes a confession of sins (CD XX.28–30) that can be compared to the one in 1QS I.24–II.1. In 1QM XIII.1–6, a series of blessing and curses can be compared with the ones in 1QS II.1–18. It is possible that the blessings included in 4QBerakhot^{a-e} (4Q286–290) should also be understood in the context of the annual covenantal ceremony. They differ somewhat from the ones in 1QS, however, and may represent a later, developed form of the ceremony (Nitzan 1994: 53–71).

Treatise on the Two Spirits

The passage containing the treatise on the two spirits (1QS III.13–IV.26) is perhaps the most analysed one in the Community Rule. The passage is distinctive indeed, for both its genre and vocabulary differ significantly from the surrounding material. The genre is wisdom literature, and the terminology of the passage reflects a dualistic, apocalyptic worldview. Commentators have observed that dualism in this passage, while framed in unflinching monotheism and bold determinism, is not consistent but manifestly pluriform: cosmic, anthropological, ethical and eschatological.

In the first part (1QS III.13–IV.14), dualism is *cosmic*, in that in the universe as established and directed by God, there are two fundamentally opposite powers, light and darkness, also identified with truth and injustice, whose mutual antagonism influences the life of human beings. The Angel of Darkness at the head of the domain of darkness controls the sons of injustice, whereas on the opposite side the Prince of Lights controls the sons of righteousness. The sons of light are not immune to the influence of the Angel of Darkness and his spirits, however, for it is they that cause the sons of light to sin.

In the second part (1QS IV.14–26) the reality of sin in the life of a righteous person is explained from an *anthropological* or *psychological* viewpoint: the two spirits battle in the heart of a human being, and depending on the person's respective portions in the realms of truth and injustice, he acts justly or wickedly. God allows this to happen, the doctrine testifies, so that human beings 'may know good and evil', and that God 'may determine the fates of every living being according to the spirit within him' (1QS IV.26). At the outset, the two halves of the doctrine appear contradictory, two separate frameworks of thought; but J. J. Collins rightly observes that 'there is a synergism between the psychological realm and the agency of the supernatural angels or demons' (1997: 41).

The dualism in the treatise on the two spirits has a strong *ethical* dimension, for considerable attention is devoted to outlining the ways in which the Spirit of Truth and the Spirit of Injustice manifest themselves in the world (1QS IV.2–14). The section contains lists of virtues and vices, and their respective rewards, and can be compared with similar lists or ethical catalogues in various Graeco-Roman, Jewish and Christian circles in antiquity. As a matter of fact, this part of the doctrine reads like 'a catechesis for people that stand on one side, light, as opposed to darkness' (Duhaime 2000: 216).

At the same time, the overall perspective of the doctrine is *eschatological*. The era of darkness will come to an end at a time appointed by God, and it will be destroyed forever (1QS IV.18-23). Those who have acted righteously will be purified with the Spirit of Truth, so that no Spirit of Injustice can remain in them. Those who have been chosen for the eternal covenant, i.e., the members of the community, will be granted heavenly wisdom and the original glory of Adam. Truth will reign in the world for ever. Thus, the four aspects, which might be seen as conflicting, are better seen as complementary.

One of the most interesting questions regarding the treatise on the two spirits in 1QS involves the background of its dualistic ideas. Can the doctrine be explained through its affinities with the Hebrew Bible and viewed as a development of biblical ideas? Does it reflect the beliefs of some specific Jewish and pre-Christian circles? Has the doctrine been affected by the dualism known from ancient Persian Zoroastrianism? Whatever its sources, are there connections with other Qumran writings? For summaries of scholarly discussion, see Philonenko 1995; Duhaime 2000: 218–20; and Collins 1997: 38–51.

There are certainly affinities with biblical traditions (e.g., Gen. 1–3; Num. 27.16; 1 Sam. 10.10; 16.14-16; 1 Kgs 22.21-23; 2 Kgs 19.7), but at the same time, the treatise contains elements alien to the Hebrew Bible – most notably the idea of conflicting forces of light and darkness, equally proportioned for a preordained period in history. Collins (1997: 41) has observed here a 'phenomenological similarity' – one found in the Enoch literature in that 'heavenly or demonic beings influence the behavior of human beings, and lead them towards a final retribution beyond this world', – but notes that there are few parallels in detail. Moreover, the origin of evil and the underlying notion of creation are different.

The dualistic motifs involving creation are linked with Zoroastrian thought as represented in the Gathas of Avesta, the ancient Persian sacred writings (esp. Yasna 30, 45 and 47). These similarities were noticed already in the early 1950s by K.-G. Kuhn (1952) and Dupont-Sommer (1952). Given the fact that the Jews were a subject people of the Persian empire for two centuries, it is by no means unlikely that certain Zoroastrian ideas had an influence on the dualism found in this treatise.

There are scholars, however, who emphasize parallels in writings geographically and historically much closer to the Qumran texts than the Avesta (Nötscher 1960: 343; Wernberg-Møller 1961: 417). Parallels to the treatise on the two spirits can be found, for example, in the book of *Jubilees* (e.g. 10), Ben Sira and *1 Enoch* (Sir. 33; 42; *1 En.* 2–5; 41–48), and in the *Testaments of the Twelve Patriarchs* (*T. Jud.* 20.1–4, *T. Ash.* 1.3–9; 3–6, *T. Benj.* 4.1–7.2). Here we may have an intricate interplay of theological ideas originating in Persian and Jewish milieus. In the early Christian writings interesting parallels are *Didache* 1–6, the *Epistle of Barnabas* 18–21 and Hermas, *Man.* 6.

The dualistic ideas of the treatise are by no means unique in the Qumran corpus, although nowhere in the Dead Sea Scrolls do we find the community's dualistic beliefs as systematically presented as in this passage in the Community Rule. Leaders at the head of opposing angelic forces, sometimes with varying names, and their influence on the behaviour of humans are discussed, for example, in the Damascus Document IV.12–VI.1; War Scroll I, XIII–XIX; 4QVisions of Amram; 11QApocryphal Psalms[a]; 11QMelchizedek; 1QH XIV.19–22 (Kobelski 1981).

The idea that the present era is under the dominion of Belial but is nearing its end, seeing that God's intervention is imminent, is similarly prominent in many texts found at Qumran, see e.g. CD VI.14; XII.22–23; 4QSongs of the Sage[a] 1.5–8.

The writings with dualistic ideas found at Qumran represent a surprising diversity in literary genre, and the dualism in these documents also manifests itself in different forms. Several studies have appeared regarding the development of Qumran dualism (see Further Reading below). With the publication of the Cave 4 material it has become increasingly apparent that the various forms of dualism with seemingly different origins were not seen to conflict with one other, nor compete to replace each other, but were able to co-exist in the Qumran corpus and work as a 'relatively coherent multidimensional system' (Duhaime 2000: 219).

Admission of New Members

The process of admitting new members into the community is discussed in several different parts of the Community Rule, including two passages describing the probationary periods and examinations a candidate must pass before becoming accepted as a full member (1QS V.20b–24 and VI.13b–23), a description of the oath to be sworn when joining the community (1QS V.7–20a), and a description of a covenantal liturgy, in which the new members were formally admitted and the membership of the existing members re-affirmed (1QS I.16–II.25). While these passages provide plenty of detail regarding the procedures of admission, it is somewhat difficult to combine these descriptions into one coherent picture. Josephus' report on the admission procedure of the Essenes (*War* II.137–9) has close affinities with the practices described in the Community Rule, but it seems to further complicate the picture.

Particularly difficult to explain is the relationship between the two passages describing the probationary periods and examinations (1QS V.20b–24 and VI.13b–23). It has been suggested that one passage simply gives a more detailed description of the same procedure than does the other (van der Ploeg 1951: 114), but a close comparison of the passages seems to indicate differences in the procedure itself: The first of the passages (V.20–23) gives the impression that full admission takes place during the first stage of examination, and the one-time decision regarding admission is made by 'the sons of Aaron and the multitude of Israel' only. The second passage (VI.13b–23) presupposes a period of probation that lasts for over two years, with gradual initiation into the practices of the community and repeated examinations: the *paqîd* (the officer in charge) is named as responsible for the initial examination of the candidate, whereas the subsequent examinations are carried out by the *rabbîm*. During the two-year probationary period, the candidate's access to the 'purity' or drink of the *rabbîm* is restricted, and his wealth is not fully pooled with the wealth of the community. The different time-frames as well as procedural differences have led some scholars argue that the two passages witness to two different stages in the community's history (Becker 1964: 42; Metso 1997: 129–33).

An additional feature complicating the comparison of these passages is that taken together, they seem to deal with more than one topic: while the focus in

VI.13b–23 is clearly the admission of the new members, in V.20b–24 not only the process of admission, but also the yearly review of the ranks of already existing members is discussed (esp. V.23–24) (Hempel 1999: 73; Metso 1997: 130). As one possibility, it has been suggested that V.20b–24 and VI.13b–23 are not thematically overlapping at all, but that the only question under discussion in the whole of V.20b–24 is the member's position in the rank, not his admission or rejection (Murphy-O'Connor 1969: 536).

Josephus' description in *War* II.137–39, although fully identical with neither of the passages mentioned above, is closer to the longer procedure reported in 1QS VI.13–23 than to the practice described in 1QS V.20–23:

> A candidate anxious to join their sect is not immediately admitted. For one year, during which he remains outside the fraternity, they prescribe for him their own rule of life, presenting him with a small hatchet, the loin-cloth already mentioned, and white raiment. Having given proof of his temperance during this probationary period, he is brought into closer touch with the rule and is allowed to share the purer kind of holy water, but is not yet received into the meetings of the community. For after this exhibition of endurance, his character is tested for two years more, and only then, if found worthy, is he enrolled in the society. But, before he may touch the common food, he is made to swear tremendous oaths (*War* II.137–39; trans. Thackeray).

Both Josephus and 1QS VI.13–23 describe an admission process that occurs in stages. But whereas Josephus speaks of an initial period of probation lasting one year that is spent outside the community, the passage in 1QS VI.13–23 does not specify the length of the initial period and appears to presume that the candidate is in some sense within the community from the very beginning. Both passages mention the candidate's closer contact with the community after the initial period, and both Josephus and 1QS VI.13–23 report a two-year period of further testing, during which the candidate's access to the common meal is restricted. The hatchet, the loin cloth and the white garments described by Josephus are not mentioned in 1QS.

The oath, however, does occur in a separate lengthy passage elsewhere in the Community Rule (1QS V.7–20). This passage during its process of textual transmission underwent particularly thorough editorial work (1QS V.7–20 // 4QS[b] IX.6–13 // 4QS[d] I.5–11; Metso 2005). All S manuscripts in which the passage is preserved agree, however, that the oath consisted of two stipulations: to return to the law of Moses and to separate from the men of injustice. Based on Josephus' report that associates the oath with the permission to touch the common food, it is possible to assume that the oath belonged to the stage described in 1QS VI.20–23 as taking place after two years of probation. The Damascus Document indicates, however, that the oath was sworn on the day the candidate offered himself for membership (CD XV.5–XVI.6, par. 4QD[a] 8 i.1–10 // 4QD[e] 6 ii.1–21 // 4QD[f] 4 ii.1–7). According to Hempel, the passage describing the oath in 1QS V.7c-9a, together with the legislation in CD XV–XVI should not be read as representative of the same time period nor the same community as the elaborate passage in 1QS VI.13–23, but as a piece of earlier communal legislation originating not in the *yaḥad* but in its parent movement, 'to which admission was gained by swearing an oath' (1999: 72).

One more passage in the Community Rule deals with the admission of new
members, but its genre is distinctly different from the passages discussed above.
In the liturgy of covenant renewal (1QS I.16–II.25), joining the community is
identified with entering into the covenant; 'covenant' has in fact obtained a
connotation of an organizational term. A series of blessings is pronounced to
those turning to follow God's commandments, while those refusing to enter the
covenant and those entering the covenant with an impure heart are cursed as
belonging to the lot of Belial. It is unclear how the ceremony should be viewed in
relation to 1QS V.20b–24, VI.13b–23 or 1QS V.7–20a, for no mention of a special ceremony of entry is made in these passages, and the dualistic language in the
liturgy is distinctly different. The ceremony may have functioned as the formal
affirmation of the admissions that had taken place during the year or, perhaps less
likely, the liturgy belongs to a period in the community's history in which
admission of new members took place only once every year.

Judicial Sessions

Two quite different passages in the Community Rule describe settings for judicial
decision-making specifically: 1QS VI.1c–8a describes the procedure for meetings
of ten members or more that take place 'in their dwelling places'(מגוריהם); 1QS
VI.8b–13a provides a rule for the session of the *rabbîm*. Questions essential for
understanding these passages are (1) whether they describe judicial decision-
making at the same or at different organizational levels and (2) whether they
mirror circumstances in the same community, or whether 1QS VI.1c–8a describes
a practice observed outside the *yaḥad* as suggested by some scholars. In addition
to these passages, certain statements in 1QS VIII–IX should be considered, especially a reference to a 'council of the community' consisting of twelve men and
three priests in 1QS VIII.1, and a reference to the authority of the sons of Aaron
in 1QS IX.7.

Material parallel to 1QS VI is preserved in 4QS[d] and 4QS[i], and material parallel to 1QS VIII–IX is preserved in 4QS[e]. The 4QS[d] fragments are parallel to 1QS
VI.1–7 and 9–12, but the 4QS[d] text appears to have been shorter than that in 1QS,
especially in the latter section. The 4QS[i] fragments are parallel to 1QS VI.1–3.
Apart from the shorter text displayed by 4QS[d] only a few variants are worth mentioning: 4QS[d] reads כוהן (a priest) where 1QS VI.3–4 has איש כוהן (a man
who is a priest). And 4QS[i] reads ול הון (wealth) where 1QS VI.2 reads ולממון
(money). This latter pair of variants seems somewhat synonymous, although ממון
is open to a negative connotation whereas הון is more neutral. As for the text of
4QS[e], surprisingly it provides a considerably shorter version of 1QS VIII–IX,
since it did not contain the lengthy passage found in 1QS VIII.15b–IX.11.

With regard to the first major passage in 1QS VI.1c–8a many commentators
have pointed out that in the context of the Community Rule it is unusual, and
seems to form an interpolation (Leaney 1966: 180; Knibb 1987: 115; Metso 1997:
115–16, 134–35; Hempel 2003: 67–68). First, it is the only passage in the Community Rule to mention the quorum of ten. Secondly, the term מגורים, derived

from the root גור meaning 'to dwell as a client', occurs nowhere else in the Rule. Thirdly, it seems strange that the point about the presence of a priest should be made at the *yaḥad*, especially when the rest of the document seems to presume rather a multitude of priests present in any given situation. Finally, the last sentence in 1QS VI.7b–8a can be seen to function as a resumptive clause and a bridge to the next passage created by the redactor.

A. R. C. Leaney suggests that the passage regulated the life of the general Essene movement in the period *before* the Qumran group withdrew to the desert, since it describes life 'as it was lived in small scattered groups, kept together by acknowledging some central authority as well as by their own community lives' (Leaney 1966: 180). M. A. Knibb is of the opinion that the material describes the circumstances *contemporary* with those at Qumran, but that the section alludes to the members of the Essene movement living in towns and villages amongst their fellow Jews (Knibb 1987: 115). These intermingled groups are mentioned by Josephus and Philo, and a basic group of ten is also referred to in the text of Josephus (*War* II.146).

J. J. Collins has discussed this passage within his larger theory of the *yaḥad* as an umbrella organization and takes a different view. Pointing out that the entire Community Rule is a compilation of small literary units, he argues that 'the passage in 1QS 6 is no more distinct literarily than other pericopes in the Rule' (2006: 87–88). He considers the groups described in 1QS VI.1–8 analogous, although not identical, to the camps in CD, and argues that these smaller communities described in 1QS VI.1–8 belonged to the *yaḥad* while 'the term *yaḥad*, as used in 1QS V.1, refers to the umbrella organization of these smaller groups, not to a single settlement such as the Qumran community' (2003:104). For a different perspective, see Metso 2006: 213–35.

The second major passage, 1QS VI.8–13, records a rule for the general assembly of the community, i.e. the session of the *rabbîm*. This section bears similarities in vocabulary to the preceding passage describing the groups of ten men, which may have been the reason why the passages were placed one after another in the Rule. Both sections use the word תכון (order, rank) in denoting the rank of members, and ordinal numbers (first, second) occur in both passages designating the order of the members (VI.5; VI.8). The purpose of both sections is to regulate how the members should behave toward each other (VI.2; VI.10), and the ways of prescribing the regulations for decision-making follow the same syntactical pattern (VI.4: 'in the same order they shall be asked their counsel in regard to any matter'; VI.9: 'in the same order they shall be asked for judgment, or concerning any counsel or matter'). The council of the community, עצת היחד, is mentioned in both passages (VI.3; VI.10), but a difference can be seen in that while the participants in the meeting taking place in the places of מגורים (dwelling places) are *from* the council of the community (מעצת היחד), the session of the *rabbîm* appears to take place *in* the council of the community (see 1QS VI.10).

Although in both passages the priests have precedence in the seating order, in VI.1c–7a the members are divided simply into two categories of priests and (lay)men, whereas in VI.8b–13 they are divided into three categories: priests, elders and the rest of the people. The procedural authority in the session of the *rabbîm* is in the hands of the *mebaqqer*, often translated as the overseer (הראיש המבקר על הרבים), but in the smaller gatherings of at least ten members, the priest is said to function as the head of the council. Unlike the rule for the session of the *rabbîm*, the rule recorded in VI.1c–7a involves not only the decision-making (the council), but other kinds of communal gatherings as well, such as prayer, the meal and the study of the law. At the common meal, as in the council, the priest takes precedence.

It is difficult to determine the relationship of these two passages to the material of 1QS VIII–IX, which also includes statements about the authority in the community. It is likely that the source for the material in 1QS VIII–IX is different from that of 1QS V–VII, and possibly describes a different time period in the community's history. According to 1QS IX.7, 'only the sons of Aaron shall rule in matters of justice and wealth, and on their word the decision shall be taken with every rule of the men of the community'. This statement appears to exclude the role given to the *mebaqqer* in 1QS VI.11–12 and seems contradictory to the picture of more democratic deliberations between the priests and the (lay)men in the groups of ten men (VI.1c–7a) and the session of the *rabbîm* (VI.8b–13).

In 1QS VIII.1 the council of the community (עצת היחד) is said to consist of twelve men and three priests. Elsewhere in the Serekh, עצת היחד is used as reference to all full members of the community (see e.g. 1QS III.2; V.7; VI.10, 13, 16; VII.2, 22–24). The question as to how the reference to a council of fifteen should be understood is disputed in the scholarly literature. Read in the context of the threefold statement 'When these exist in Israel' (see VIII.4, 12; IX.3) and the highly idealistic language of 1QS VIII–IX, some consider it as designating the founders of the community who withdrew to the desert to live a life of holiness according to the Mosaic law (Sutcliffe 1959; Murphy-O'Connor 1969: 529; Knibb 1987: 129). Others view it as an inner council of leaders (Baumgarten 1976: 64; Stegemann 1998: 158) or an elite group within the *yaḥad* (Collins 2003: 105). Compounding the confusion is the quite different possibility first mentioned by Milik that the number fifteen in 1QS VIII.1 may have been used symbolically, in order to create a link with the twelve tribes of Israel and three priestly families (Milik 1959: 100).

The passages describing judicial sessions in the Community Rule have affinities with a number of texts found at Qumran. The section in 1QS VI.1–8 mentioning groups of ten can be compared with a similar section in CD XII.22–XIII.7 for camps consisting of a minimum of ten members. Another group of ten, namely ten judges of the congregation (שפטי העדה) is mentioned in CD X.4. In 1QSa II.22 the procedure describing the messianic banquet ends with the statement: 'It is in accordance with this statute that they shall proceed at every me[al at which] at least ten men [g]ather', thus creating a link between the messianic age and the meal practices of the community. The rule for the session of the *rabbîm* in 1QS VI.8–13, for its part, can be compared with CD XIV.3–18, a section entitled the 'rule for those who live in all the camps' that includes a specific rule for the *rabbîm* (XIV.12–17).

For 1QS VIII.1–12 and its reference to the twelve men and three priests, a significant parallel can be found in 4QpIsa[d], that speaks of 'the priests and the people' as those who founded (or will found) the council of the community (ויסדו את עצת היחד [ה]כוהנים והע[ם...]). Although the text is fragmentary, the numeral 'twelve' also appears in the context. A more extensive parallel, with significant overlaps of 1QS VIII.1–8, is preserved in 4Q265 frg. 7. It is possible that there is direct literary dependency between these passages, or that they share a common source.

Penal Codes

In the Essene community, what was required was no less than 'perfection of way', that is, perfect conduct (e.g. 1QS I.8; II.2; VIII. 21; IX.5). The penal codes preserved in the Qumran corpus attest, however, that human failings were not alien to the members of the community. Few other parts of the Essene library illustrate as vividly and authentically the demands of an ascetic life as the penal codes. Two different sets of penal regulations are included in the Community Rule: 1QS VI.24–VII.25 (partial parallels in 4QS[d,e,g]) and VIII.16b–IX.2 (partial parallels in 4QS[d]). These can be compared with other penal codes included in the Qumran corpus: 4QD[a] frg. 10, 4QD[d] frg. 11, and 4Q265. They also bear similarities with the penal codes of ancient Graeco-Roman voluntary associations, as M. Weinfeld (1986) has shown.

Both penal codes included in 1QS are clear about the *rabbîm* having the authority in the judicial cases of the community (VII.21; VIII.19; IX.2). They differ, however, in the way these cases are described in the two codes. The first passage (VI.24–VII.25) pinpoints detailed offences and stipulates detailed punishments: 'If a man is found among them who has knowingly lied about wealth, they shall exclude him from the purity of the *rabbîm* for one year, and he shall do penance with respect to one quarter of his food (VI.24–25)'. In contrast, the second passage (1QS VIII.16b–IX.2) describes violations and punishments in very general terms: 'No man among the men of the covenant of the community, who presumptuously leaves unfulfilled any one of the commands shall touch the purity of the men of the holiness or know any of their commands' (VIII.16b–18a). How long the punishment should last, is not told in advance, but the transgression is seen to be atoned for, when 'his deeds have been cleansed from all injustice, so that he walks in perfection of way' (VIII.18b). The criteria for being cleansed are not determined. There is merely a statement that the *rabbîm* should make the decision of reversing the previous status of the member (VIII.19). Thus, there are clear stylistic differences between the two penal codes in how the transgressions and their punishments are characterized. It is clear that the two penal codes do not belong to a unified set of regulations.

A further indication that the penal codes were likely to have been compiled from materials that did not originally belong together is apparent through comparison between VIII.16b–19 and VIII.21b–23a. The first prescribes a temporary punishment, whereas the second prescribes a permanent punishment seemingly for the same offense. In VIII.16b–19, 'no man among the men of the covenant of the community, who presumptuously leaves unfulfilled any one of the commands shall touch the purity of the men of the holiness or know any of their commands, *until his deeds have been cleansed from all injustice by walking in perfection of way*'. In contrast, VIII.21b–23a states: 'Every man of them who transgresses a word from the law of Moses presumptuously or negligently *shall be sent away from the council of the community and shall never return*'. For further discussion on these two passages, see Knibb 1987: 136 and Metso 1997: 126–28.

The 26 diverse cases listed in the code of 1QS VI.24–VII.25 occur in no particular order. For example, the similar offenses of insulting and slandering another person, which similarly lead to exclusion and penance for a period of one year, are placed in two different parts (VII.4–5; VII.15–16). Nor does the severity of the transgression seem to have played a role in the order of the code, for two offenses both of which lead to a ten-day fine (the exact nature of which is unclear), namely interruption of speech (1QS VII.9–10) and gesticulation with the left hand (1QS VII.15), are placed apart from each other in the list of transgressions.

The literary genre of the list is that of casuistic law, which has its prototype in the Hebrew Bible, especially in the Book of the Covenant (Exod. 20.22–23.33). The formulations of this type of law respond to 'but what if' type of questions posed to the legal community, as is evident from the following passage: 'Whoever (וֹאֲשֶׁר) speaks deceitfully to his neighbor or knowingly acts deceitfully shall do penance for six months. If (וֹאִם) he is negligent towards his neighbour, he shall do penance for three months. But if (וֹאִם) he is negligent with regard to the wealth of the community so that he causes its loss, he shall restore it in full. If (וֹאִם) he is unable to restore it, he shall do penance for sixty days (VII.5b–8).'

The transgressions vary from very serious – blasphemy, slandering the *rabbîm*, murmuring against the foundations of the community, and leaving the community after a ten-year membership – to trivial – such as falling asleep and spitting in the meeting of the *rabbîm*. It is interesting to note that in the Community Rule ritual impurity and moral impurity are undifferentiated. Any impurity, whether ritual or moral, tainted a person; a process of purification was required to release the offender and reunite him to the purity of the community.

The penalties also vary, with three levels stipulated in the penal codes of the Community Rule: expulsion (לוֹא יָשׁוּב עוֹד + הבדיל), exclusion (מובדל/הבדיל), penance or fine (נענש). Additionally, in one case, losing communal property, there is also the possibility of compensation (שׁלם pi.). Whereas the first is clear, the exact meaning of the second and third is not fully clear. 'Exclusion' cancelled the member's right to 'touch the purity (טהרה) of the *rabbîm*'. Although it is not certain, some propose that it primarily involved a ban on participation in the cultic meals of the community (Lieberman 1952: 203; Metso 1997: 126; Vermes 2004: 33). The content of 'penance' is clear only in its first occurrence in the text (VI.25): cutting the food ration by one quarter. Whether the meaning of נענש is the same later in the text when the term appears alone without any further definitions, remains questionable. No other explanations, however, have been proposed.

The numerous corrections and erasures made by a second scribe in 1QS VII attest that the penal regulations in the community were subject to change and development. Originally in VII.8 the punishment for bearing a grudge against one's neighbour was 'six months', but the second scribe wrote 'one year' above it, substituting a more severe penalty. A second example is highlighted by comparison of 1QS VII.14 with 4QS^e I.13: in 4QS^e, the punishment for letting one's nakedness be seen lasts sixty days, whereas in 1QS VII.14 it lasts only thirty days. Since the relative age of the textual traditions in 4QS^e and in 1QS is debated, it is difficult to determine on the basis of these two examples alone, whether there was a general tendency in one direction, towards more lenient or more severe punishments, or whether each case may have been re-evaluated on its own.

The Damascus Document displays an important parallel to the penal code of 1QS VII in two manuscripts, 4QD^a (4Q266) and 4QD^e (4Q270). The parallel passages (1QS VII.8–21; 4QD^a 10 ii.2–15; and 4QD^e 7 i.1–10) include sixteen cases of transgression plus punishment. Thirteen occur both in the Community Rule and in the Damascus Document, and they occur in identical order. Three additional cases, however, are included in 1QS, interspersed among the commonly shared regulations. Absent from the Damascus Document but included in the Community Rule are cases concerning revenge for oneself, spitting in the meeting of the *rabbîm*, and murmuring against the foundations of the community.

A unique feature of the Damascus Document is its use of double punishments consisting of exclusion and fine/penance, which appears in five cases: insulting the neighbour, foolish speech, falling asleep at the meeting of the *rabbîm*, indecent exposure and deviating from the fundamental principles of the community. The relative severity or triviality of the offence does not seem to be a factor in eliciting a double punishment, since the phenomenon appears both for deviating from the fundamental principles of the community and for foolish speech. What is significant, however, is that in every case the length of the *exclusion* in 4QD corresponds to the length of the *fine* in 1QS.

Those who have compared the penal codes in D and S generally agree that neither document directly borrowed the material from the other (Baumgarten 1992; 1996: 7–9, 74–75, 162–66; Hempel 1997; Metso 2000a). The differences between them suggest that both are dependent upon a common source, and both subsequently appear to have undergone redaction independently of each other.

A final important parallel for the penal code in 1QS is found in 4Q265, frg. 4 i–ii. Its text is preserved only fragmentarily, and what restorations there are, as the editor of the manuscript, J. Baumgarten writes (1999: 65), are largely derived from 1QS VI–VII. But it appears to have included parallels to seven of the cases in 1QS VI–VII, though in a different order. Moreover, double punishments similar to those in 4QD are attested in 4Q265, but they vary in duration and severity.

Excursus: Officials in the Community

The Community Rule mentions three specially appointed officials central to the administration of the priestly and lay membership of the community (i.e. *yaḥad*):

maskîl, paqîd and *mebaqqer*, often translated as 'wise leader', 'examiner' and 'overseer'. Based on the text of the Community Rule alone, their exact roles and duties in the community are somewhat difficult to determine. However, they are mentioned in other rule texts found at Qumran as well, and comparison with these texts both gives a fuller picture and also complicates the situation. Indeed the duties of these officials are described differently in different documents: that is, the names of the officials are the same, but the tasks attributed to the officials differ from one document to another.

Maskîl (משכיל)

Both the Community Rule and the Damascus Document mention the *maskîl*. Some scholars interpret the term in the way it is understood in the book of Daniel (11.33; 12.3), that is, they understand it in its general use 'wise man'. Most, however, interpret it as referring to a specific community official, and their interpretation seems confirmed by statements in 1QS IX.12, III.13 and 1QSb I.1, III.22, V.20. A different question is whether the *maskîl* is a layperson or a priest. J. Hempel (1963: 197), Knibb (1987: 96) and K. Koenen (1993: 794) view him as lay. One of his functions, however, apparently requires rather that he be a priest or a Levite (note also the occurrence of 2 Chron. 30.22: כל הלוים המשכילים). 1QSb (I.1; III.22; V.20) stipulates that the *maskîl* is to bless the God-fearing, the priests and the prince of the congregation. But according to 1QS I.16–II.18 only priests and Levites, never laymen, act as those who pronounce blessings and curses, indicating that the *maskîl* was either a priest or a Levite. Moreover, in 4Q510 and 4Q511 the *maskîl* has the function of reciting protective hymns against evil spirits, again pointing to a priest or a Levite.

Among the principal tasks addressed to the *maskîl* in the Community Rule is to 'instruct and teach all the sons of light' about the treatise on the two spirits (1QS III.13). This educational duty assigned to him is well in line with the statements in two other major sections in the Rule (1QS IX.12–21a; IX.21b–26) that stress his role as a spiritual teacher and leader. His charge was to lead new members into the secrets of the interpretation of the law (1QS IX.14, 17–18) and to ensure that the secrets remain within the community, hidden from outsiders (IX.16–20). He was also to 'separate and weigh the sons of righteousness according to their spirit' (IX.14), perhaps both novices and members whose rank needed reinstatement (IX.12, 15, 17–18). The Rule required his absolute commitment to the will and law of God (IX.13, 23).

Paqîd and Mebaqqer (פקיד and מבקר)

The Community Rule and the Damascus Document mention two other officials *paqîd* 'examiner' and *mebaqqer* 'overseer'. In the Community Rule, unlike the *maskîl*, they do not have a special set of rules, but are mentioned in 1QS VI only in passing, in passages describing the function of the *rabbîm*, that is, the general council of the community. The *paqîd* is the leader of the *rabbîm*, and his function was to examine those who seek to become members of the community and to teach them the community's rules (1QS VI.14–15). Confusingly, according to a nearby passage (VI.12), the *mebaqqer* also appears to be the leader of the *rabbîm*. He is charged with administering the property of the candidates during their second year of probation (VI.20).

Since both the *mebaqqer* and *paqîd* are described as leader of the *rabbîm*, does this mean that they are one and the same official with two functions or might they be two separate officials with overlapping duties? The majority opinion gravitates, though hesitantly, toward viewing the two terms as designating a single official because of clues in the Damascus Document.

Whereas CD XV.8 (just as 1QS VI.12) speaks of the *mebaqqer* of the *rabbîm* (המבקר אשר לרבים), CD XIII.7–11 further adds that the *mebaqqer* is the head of the camp whose duty it is to teach the *rabbîm*. He is charged with teaching the *rabbîm* as well as with examining the candidates, but the verb used for 'examine' is *pqd* (see also 1QS VI.14). It is due to this intermingling of terms that most view these offices as one. There is a range of other views, including that the *paqîd* was a priest, but the *mebaqqer* a lay leader (Milik 1959: 99–100; Priest 1962: 55–61), and that the *mebaqqer* should be identified with the *maskîl* (Vermes 2004: 28–29). This last view runs into the difficulty that in the Community Rule the *maskîl* appears only as the spiritual teacher and leader of the community, and never as an administrative officer.

Further Reading

Alexander, P. S., 'Physiognomy, Initiation, and Rank in the Qumran Community', in H. Cancik, H. Lichtenberger and P. Schäfer (eds), *Geschichte–Tradition–Reflexion: Festschrift für Martin Hengel zum 70. Geburtstag*, vol. 1 (Tübingen: Mohr-Siebeck, 1996), pp. 385–94.

Baumgarten, J. M., 'The Duodecimal Courts of Qumran, Revelation, and the Sanhedrin', *JBL* 95 (1976), pp. 59–78.

—'The Cave 4 Versions of the Qumran Penal Code', *JJS* 43 (1992), pp. 268–76.

Beall, T. S., *Josephus' Description of the Essenes Illustrated by the Dead Sea Scrolls* (SNTSMS, 58; Cambridge: Cambridge University Press, 1988).

Becker, J., *Das Heil Gottes: Heils- und Sündenbegriffe in den Qumrantexten und im Neuen Testament* (SUNT, 3; Göttingen: Vandenhoeck & Ruprecht, 1964).

Bernstein, M. J., 'Hymn on Occasions for Prayer (1QS 10:8b–17)', in M. C. Kiley *et al.* (eds), *Prayer from Alexander to Constantine: A Critical Anthology* (London: Routledge, 1997), pp. 33–37.

Charlesworth, J. H., 'Community Organization in the Rule of the Community', in L. H. Schiffman and J. C. VanderKam, *Encyclopedia of the Dead Sea Scrolls* (Oxford: Oxford University Press, 2000), pp. 133–36.

Collins, J. J., *Apocalypticism in the Dead Sea Scrolls* (The Literature of the Dead Sea Scrolls, 1; London: Routledge, 1997).

—'The Construction of Israel in the Sectarian Rule Books', in J. Neusner, A. J. Avery-Peck and B. Chilton, *Judaism in Late Antiquity*, vol. 3 (Leiden: Brill, 2001), pp. 25–42.

—'Forms of Community in the Dead Sea Scrolls', in S. M. Paul *et al.* (eds), *Emanuel: Studies in Hebrew Bible, Septuagint, and Dead Sea Scrolls in Honor of Emanuel Tov* (Leiden: Brill, 2003), pp. 97–111.

—'The Yaḥad and "The Qumran Community"', in C. Hempel and J. M. Lieu (eds), *Biblical Traditions in Transmission: Essays in Honour of Michael A. Knibb* (JSJSup, 111; Leiden: Brill, 2006), pp. 81–96.

Conway, C. M. 'Toward a Well-formed Subject: the Function of Purity Language in the Serek ha-Yaḥad', *JSP* 21 (2000), pp. 103–20.

Delcor, M., 'Doctrines des Esséniens. I. L'Instruction des deux esprits', *DBSup* 9 (Paris: Letouzey et Ané, 1979), pp. 960–70.

Destro, A. and M. Pesce, 'The Gospel of John and the Community Rule of Qumran: A Comparison of Systems', in J. Neusner, A. J. Avery-Peck and B. Chilton, *Judaism in Late Antiquity*, vol. 3 (Leiden: Brill, 2001), pp. 201–29.

Duhaime, J., 'L'instruction sur les deux esprits et les interpolations dualistes à Qumrân', *RB* 84 (1977), pp. 566–94.

—'Dualism', in L. H. Schiffman and J. C. VanderKam (eds), *Encyclopedia of the Dead Sea Scrolls*, vol. 1 (Oxford: Oxford University Press, 2000), pp. 215–20.

Dupont-Sommer A., 'L'instruction sur les deux Esprits dans le "Manuel de Discipline"', *RHR* 142 (1952), pp. 5–35.

Falk, D. K., *Daily, Sabbath, and Festival Prayers in the Dead Sea Scrolls* (STDJ, 27; Leiden: Brill, 1998).

Fraade, S. D., 'Interpretive Authority in the Studying Community at Qumran', *JJS* 44 (1993), pp. 46–69.

García Martínez, F., 'Priestly Functions in a Community without Temple', in B. Ego, A. Lange and P. Pilhofer (eds), *Gemeinde ohne Temple: Community without Temple* (WUNT, 118; Tübingen: Mohr-Siebeck, 1999), pp. 303–19.

Hempel, C., 'The Penal Code Reconsidered', in M. Bernstein, F. García Martínez and J. Kampen (eds), *Legal Texts and Legal Issues: Proceedings of the Second Meeting of the International Organization for Qumran Studies, Cambridge 1995* (Leiden: Brill, 1997) 337–48.

—'Community Structures in the Dead Sea Scrolls: Admission, Organization, Disciplinary Procedures', in P. W. Flint and J. C. VanderKam (eds), *The Dead Sea Scrolls after Fifty Years: A Comprehensive Assessment*, vol. 2 (Leiden: Brill, 1999), pp. 67–92.

—'Interpretative Authority in the Community Rule Tradition', *DSD* 10 (2003), pp. 59–80.

Hempel, J., 'Die Stellung des Laien in Qumran', in H. Bardtke (ed.), *Qumran-Probleme: Vorträge des leipziger Symposions über Qumran-Probleme vom 9. bis 14. Oktober 1961* (Berlin: Akademie Verlag, 1963), pp. 193–215.

Jokiranta, J., ' "Sectarianism" of the Qumran "Sect": Sociological Notes', *RevQ* 20 (2001), pp. 223–39.

Klinghardt, M., *Gemeinschaftsmahl und Mahlgemeinschaft: Soziologie und Liturgie früh-christlicher Mahlfeiern* (Texte und Arbeiten zum neutestamentlichen Zeitalter, 13; Tübingen: Francke Verlag, 1996).

Knibb, M. A., *The Qumran Community* (Cambridge Commentaries on Writings of the Jewish and Christian World 200 BC to AD 200, 2; Cambridge: Cambridge University Press, 1987).

Kobelski, P. J., *Melchizedek and Melchiresha'* (Washington, D.C.: Catholic Biblical Association, 1981).

Krasovec, J., 'Sources of Confession of Sin in 1QS 1:24–26 and CD 20:28–30', in L. H. Schiffman, E. Tov and J. C. VanderKam, *The Dead Sea Scrolls Fifty Years After Their Discovery* (Jerusalem: Israel Exploration Society/Shrine of the Book Museum, Israel, 2000), pp. 306–21.

Kugler, R. A., 'A Note on 1QS 9.14: The Sons of Righteousness or the Sons of Zadok?', *DSD* 3 (1996), pp. 315–20.

Kuhn, H.-W., *Enderwartung und gegenwärtiges Heil* (Göttingen: Vandenhoeck & Ruprecht, 1966).

Kuhn, K.-G., 'Die Sektenschrift und die iranische Religion', *ZTK* 49 (1952), pp. 296–316.

Lange, A., *Weisheit und Prädestination: Weisheitliche Urordnung und Prädestination in den Textfunden von Qumran* (STDJ, 18; Leiden: Brill, 1995).

Lieberman, S., 'The Discipline in the So-called Dead Sea Manual of Discipline', *JBL* 71 (1952), 199–206.

Metso, S., *The Textual Development of the Qumran Community Rule* (STDJ, 21: Leiden: Brill, 1997).

—'The Relationship Between the Damascus Document and the Community Rule', in J. M. Baumgarten, E. G. Chazon and A. Pinnick (eds), *The Damascus Document: A Centennial of Discovery. Proceedings of the Third International Symposium of the Orion Center, 4–8 February, 1998* (STDJ, 34; Leiden: Brill, 2000), pp. 85–93.

—'Creating Community Halakhah', in P. W. Flint, E. Tov and J. C. VanderKam (eds), *Studies in the Hebrew Bible, Qumran, and the Septuagint: Presented to Eugene Ulrich* (Leiden: Brill, 2005), pp. 279–301.

—'Whom Does the Term *Yaḥad* Identify?', in C. Hempel and J. Lieu (eds), *Biblical Traditions in Transmission: Essays in Honour of Michael A. Knibb* (JSJSup, 11; Leiden: Brill, 2006), pp. 213–235.

Milik, J. T., *Ten Years of Discovery in the Wilderness of Judaea* (trans. J. Strugnell [*Dix ans de découvertes dans le Désert de Juda*; Paris: Cerf, 1957]; SBT, 26; London: SCM Press, 1959).

Newsom, C. A., *The Self as Symbolic Space: Constructing Identity and Community at Qumran* (STDJ, 52; Leiden: Brill, 2004).

Nitzan, B., *Qumran Prayer and Religious Poetry* (trans. J. Chipman; STDJ, 12; Leiden: Brill, 1994) esp. pp. 125–139.

—'4Q Berakhot (4Q286–290): A Preliminary Report', in G. J. Brooke and F. García Martínez, *New Qumran Texts and Studies: Proceedings of the First Meeting of the International Organization for Qumran Studies, Paris 1992* (Leiden: Brill, 1994), pp. 53–71.

—'The Laws of Reproof in 4QBerakhot (4Q286–290) in Light of their Parallels in the Damascus Covenant and other Texts from Qumran', in M. Bernstein, F. García Martínez and J. Kampen (eds), *Legal Texts and Legal Issues: Proceedings of the Second Meeting of the International Organization for Qumran Studies, Cambridge 1995* (STDJ, 23; Leiden: Brill, 1997), pp. 149–65.

Osten-Sacken, P. von der, *Gott und Belial: Traditionsgeschichtliche Untersuchungen zum Dualismus in den Texten aus Qumran* (SUNT, 6; Göttingen: Vandenhoeck & Ruprecht, 1969).

Philonenko, M., 'La doctrine qoumrânienne des deux esprits: Ses origins iraniennes et ses prolongements dans le judaïsme essénien et le christianisme antique', in G. Widengren, A. Hultgård and M. Philonenko, *Apocalyptique iranienne et dualisme qoumrânien* (Reserches intertestamentaires, 2; Paris: Maisonneuve, 1995), pp. 163–211.

Priest, J. F., 'Mebaqqer, Paqid, and the Messiah', *JBL* 81 (1962), pp. 55–61.

Schiffman, L. H., *Sectarian Law in the Dead Sea Scrolls: Courts, Testimony and the Penal Code* (BJS, 33; Chico, CA: Scholars Press, 1983).

—*Reclaiming the Dead Sea Scrolls: The History of Judaism, the Background of Christianity, the Lost Library of Qumran* (Philadelphia and Jerusalem: The Jewish Publication Society, 1994), esp. pp. 97–105.

—'Community without Temple: the Qumran Community's Withdrawal from the Jerusalem Temple', in B. Ego, A. Lange and P. Pilhofer (eds), *Community without Temple* (WUNT, 118; Tübingen: Mohr-Siebeck, 1999), pp. 267–84.

Stuckenbruck, L., 'Wisdom and Holiness at Qumran: Strategies for Dealing with Sin in the Community Rule', in S. C. Barton (ed.), *Where Shall Wisdom be Found?* (Edinburgh: T&T Clark, 1999), pp. 47–60.

Sutcliffe, E.F., 'The First Fifteen Members of the Qumran Community: A Note on 1QS 8:1 ff.', *JSS* 4 (1959), pp. 134–38.

VanderKam, J. C., *Calendars in the Dead Sea Scrolls: Measuring Time* (The Literature of the Dead Sea Scrolls; London: Routledge, 1998).

—'Identity and History of the Community', in P. W. Flint and J. C. VanderKam (eds), *The Dead Sea Scrolls After Fifty Years: A Comprehensive Assessment*, vol. 2 (Leiden: Brill, 1999), pp. 487–533.

—'The Judean Desert and the Community of the Dead Sea Scrolls', in B. Kollmann, W. Reinbold and A. Steudel (eds), *Antikes Judentum und frühes Christentum: Festschrift für Hartmut Stegemann zum 65. Geburtstag* (Beihefte zur Zeitschrift für die neutestamentliche Wissenschaft, 97; Berlin: de Gruyter, 1999), pp. 159–71.

Vermes, G., 'The Leadership of the Qumran Community: Sons of Zadok–Priests–Congregation', in H. Cancik, H. Lichtenberger and P. Schäfer (eds), *Geschichte–Tradition–Reflexion: Festschrift für Martin Hengel zum 70. Geburtstag*, vol. 1 (Tübingen: J. C. B. Mohr [Paul Siebeck], 1996), pp. 375–84.

Weinfeld, M., *The Organizational Pattern and the Penal Code of the Qumran Sect: A Comparison with Guilds and Religious Associations of the Hellenistic-Roman Period* (NTOA, 2; Göttingen: Vandenhoeck & Ruprecht, 1986).

Weise, M., *Kultzeiten und kultischer Bundesschluss in der 'Ordensregel' vom Toten Meer* (SPB, 3; Leiden: Brill, 1961).

Chapter 5

THE COMMUNITY RULE AND THE BIBLE

The Use of the Hebrew Bible in the Community Rule

The world and language of the Hebrew Bible permeates the entire Qumran corpus, so it is not surprising that implicitly, the Community Rule echoes the Scriptures almost constantly. Scriptural phrases and expressions have been worked into the very fabric of the text without being designated as citations. This kind of anthological style, seen in other Qumran texts, and in the New Testament as well, shows thorough saturation in and prolonged meditation on the Scriptures. Isolated explicit citations of Scripture introduced by specific formulae are far less frequent in the Community Rule. In 1QS there are only three of them and, quite astonishingly, in 4QS^{b,d} they are entirely lacking.

In the case of the so-called rule texts (1QS, CD, 1QM) we are dealing with writings very different from the exegetical texts belonging to the interpretative genre, which includes on the one hand such thematic midrashim as 4QMidrEschat (4Q174+177) and 11QMelchizedek, and on the other the systematic pesharim commentaries on complete biblical books. Whereas these exegetical writings display a clearly recognizable structure and take the citation as a starting-point for the interpretation, the structure in the rule texts varies and citations are inserted rather to support or illustrate an argument. Very often a citation acts as a kind of proof-text, and this is the case with the quotations we find in the Community Rule, as they are used to bolster and justify the need for separation from outsiders. Within the Qumran writings the rule-texts (1QS, CD, 1QM), which combine citations into a prose narrative, come closest to the way the citations are used in the New Testament.

Two of the three scriptural citations in 1QS are found in column V, which begins a collection of rules for community life. A passage commencing in line 7 speaks about the oath to be taken by those desiring to become members of the community. They are to bind themselves to the law of Moses (1QS V.7b–10a) and to separate from the men of injustice (1QS V.10b–20a). In 1QS V.7 the passage has a clear title: 'These are their rules of conduct, according to all these statutes, when they are admitted to the community', while 4QS^{b,d} lacks a title and simply begins with the words 'Everyone who joins the council of the community …'. A brief glimpse at the two versions in contrast reveals that the text of 1QS is more than twice as long as that of 4QS^{b,d}. In the following translation, the parts where the versions clearly differ from each other in content are in italics.

1QS V.13b–16a

4QS[b] IX.8b–10a:

> (8b) [They shall not touch the purity of of the men] (9) of holiness. *He shall not eat with him within the community.*
>
> No one [of the men of the community shall answer to their authority] (10) with regard to any law or decision.

4QS[d] I.7b–9a:

> (7b) They shall not touch the purity of of the men (8) of [holin]ess. *He shall not eat with him within [the community.*
>
> No one of the me]n of the community shall answer to their authority with regard to any (9a) [law] or decision.

1QS V.13b–16a:

> (13b) He shall not enter the waters in order to touch the purity of the men of holiness, *for men are not purified (14) unless they turn from the evil; for he remains unclean amongst all the transgressors of his word. No one shall join with him with regard to his work or his wealth lest he burden him (15) with iniquity and guilt (cf. Lev. 22.15-16). But he shall keep away from him in everything, for thus it is written, 'You shall keep away from everything false' (Exod 23.7).*
>
> No one of the men of the community shall answer (16a) to their authority with regard to any law or decision. (trans. Knibb)

Though the beginning of the passage is roughly similar in the two forms of the text (1QS and 4QS[b,d]), in 1QS V.13b–15a there is a section which is completely lacking in 4QS[b,d]. In this passage in 1QS the basic statement of the oath to separate oneself from outsiders is clarified and confirmed with biblical proof-texts – Lev. 22.15-16 and Exod. 23.7. The first is cited implicitly (ולא ... והשיאו אותם עון אשמה 'No one ... and burden them with iniquity requiring a guilt offering', Lev. 22.15-16). But the second is a direct quotation: an introduction formula כיא כן כתוב ('For thus it is written'), announces the quotation from Exodus, מכול דבר שקר תרחק ('You shall keep away from everything false', Exod. 23.7). Actually Exodus 23.7 has to do with justice in law-suits, but here – typically for Qumran exegesis – it has been disconnected from its original context and applied to an entirely different matter. The catchwords here are דבר and רחק. The word דבר occurs not only immediately before the citation formula but also earlier in line 14, in the third of five sentences starting with the conjunction כיא (note that this series of five consecutive sentences beginning with כיא is unusual and is a result of redactional development).

1QS V.16b–19a

4QS[b] IX.10b–12a:

> (10b) No man among (11) the men of holiness shall eat [...]
> [They shall not rely on any deeds of vanity, for vanity are al]l those who do not [know (12a) his covenant....]

4QS^d I.9b–11a:

> (9b) No man among the men of holiness shall eat (10) […]
> They shall not rely on a[ny dee]ds of vanity, for vanity are all those who [do not
> know 11a his covenant….]

1QS V.16b–19a:

> (16b) No one shall eat *or drink anything of their property, or take anything at all
> from their hand, (17) except for payment, as it is written, 'Have no more to do
> with man in whose nostrils is breath, for what is he worth? (Isa. 2.22)' For (18)
> all those who are not counted in his covenant, they and everything that belongs to
> them are to be kept separate.*
>
> No man of holiness shall rely on any deeds (19a) of vanity, for vanity are all those
> who do not know his covenant. (trans. Knibb)

As in the previous example, the two forms of the *Serekh* have a similar beginning.
1QS has a passage containing a biblical quotation not in 4QS^{b,d}, and then the two
forms resume their common text. As in the previous example, the passage stipulates a prohibition against contact with the men of injustice, apparently with the
concern to preserve the ritual purity of the community. The formula preceding
the citation here is slightly different from the one in the previous passage. Instead
of כיא בן כתוב ('for thus it is written') the text of 1QS reads כאשר כתוב ('as it
is written'). The quotation is followed by an interpretive comment. Note that in
the context of the previous citation such an expository element is lacking.
Obviously, the writer played with the verb נחשב 'be accounted, be esteemed' and
twisted its sense to bear the meaning 'being reckoned in the community' (cf. the
occurrence of the same verb in 1QS V.11). In the MT form of Isaiah this verse,
which according to many commentators is actually a gloss (note that it is absent
from LXX), counsels the people to cease trusting in the proud man, for in the day
of God's judgement human pride will be humbled. In 1QS the warning of Isaiah
has been turned into a sort of precept concerning an entirely different matter.

1QS VIII.12b–16a

4QS^d VI.6b–8a:

> (6b) When these exist [in Israel], they shall separate themselves f[rom the settle-
> ment of (7) the men of injustice and shall go into the wilderness to prepare there
> the way of truth (? 1QS: of him). This is the study of the la]w which he com-
> manded thro[ugh Moses, that they should d]o all [that has been revealed (8a) from
> time to time and in accordance with what the prophets revealed by his holy spirit.

1QS VIII.12b–16a:

> When these exist *as a community* in Israel (13) *in accordance with these rules,*
> they shall separate themselves from the settlement of the men of injustice and
> shall go into the wilderness to prepare there the way of him, (14) *as it is written:*
> *'In the wilderness prepare the way of* ••••, *make level in the desert a highway for*
> *our God (Isa. 40.3).'* (15) This (way) is the study of the law w[hich] he commanded
> through Moses, that they should act in accordance with all that has been revealed
> from time to time 16a and in accordance with what the prophets revealed by his
> holy spirit. (trans. Knibb)

This third example will be discussed below in the next section on the New Testament.

The evidence of these three biblical citations indicates that 1QS presents a secondary redaction of an earlier form of the Community Rule as attested in 4QS^{b,d}. The redaction was designed both to provide legitimization from Scripture for the community's rules and to strengthen the community's self-understanding. A possible motive for adding the proof-texts is that enthusiasm within the community may have begun to decrease and the need for separation may have been questioned. Thus the authoritativeness of the ascetic regulations was justified by appeal to the Torah and the Prophets. For a fuller discussion on the quotations and how the use of quotations serves to indicate redactional development within the textual traditions of the Community Rule, see Metso 2002.

The Community Rule and the New Testament

The Community Rule is a document that records the beliefs and rules of the Essene community living at Khirbet Qumran near the Dead Sea at the period before, during and after the life of Jesus of Nazareth. It is important not only for understanding the Essenes, but also for shedding light on the New Testament at many significant points. Several areas can be mentioned where it is fruitful to compare the New Testament material with the Community Rule.

'Preparing the Way of the Lord'
The Qumranites used a verse from the Book of Isaiah to provide a rationale for the community's withdrawal into the desert to live a life of perfection in accordance with the law. The text of the Community Rule reads: 'When these exist as a community in Israel in accordance with these rules, they shall separate themselves from the settlement of the men of injustice and shall go into the wilderness to prepare there the way of [the Lord], as it is written: In the wilderness prepare the way of the Lord, make level in the desert a highway for our God'. The same verse from Isaiah 40.3 is also used in the New Testament with reference to John the Baptist by all four evangelists (Mt. 3.3; Mk 1.3, Lk. 3.4–6, Jn 1.23). Deutero-Isaiah's original proclamation was that Yahweh was about to put himself at the head of his people and lead them to freedom from exile across the desert, as he had done at the exodus from Egypt into the Promised Land. Both the Community Rule and the four evangelists have in analogous ways disregarded the historical context, detached the verse from its original meaning and adapted the words to fit into their new environments – the Qumran community for its self-identity to explain its withdrawal into the desert, and the evangelists to explain John the Baptist's proclamation of the coming Lord, identified with Jesus, while baptizing in the desert.

Concepts and Theological Ideas
Secondly, there are many concepts and theological ideas held in common by the Community Rule and the New Testament. The strongly dualistic language of the

treatise on the two spirits (1QS III.13–IV.26) has similarities with the ethical and eschatological dualism in the Gospel of John:

> God created man to rule all the world, and he assigned two spirits to him that he might walk by them until the appointed time of his visitation; they are the spirits of truth and of injustice. From a spring of light come the generations of truth, and from a well of darkness the generations of injustice. Control over all the sons of righteousness lies in the hand of the prince of lights, and they walk in the ways of light; complete control over the sons of injustice lies in the hand of the angel of darkness, and they walk in the ways of darkness. (1QS III.17–21; trans. M. Knibb)

For the opposition of light and darkness in John, see, e.g. Jn 1.4-5; 3.19; 12.35-36 (cf. also 1 Jn 1.5-6) and for the opposition of truth and falsehood, see, e.g. Jn 3.21; 8.44 (cf. also 1 Jn 2.21, 27; 4.6). But though some parallels are striking (e.g., 'Spirit of Truth' in Jn 14.17; 15.26; 16.13 and 1QS III.18–19; IV.21, 23; 'sons of light' in Jn 12.36 and 1QS III.13, 24, 25), Johannine dualism – in which Jesus is truth incarnate – is not identical with that of the Essenes – for whom the truth is revealed in the Torah. In fact, dualistic thinking is broadly attested in Judaism and later Christianity. In Jewish texts it can be seen in *Jubilees* 10, Sirach 33, *1 Enoch* 2–5 and 41–48, and *Testaments of the Twelve Patriarchs* (*T. Jud.* 20.1-4; *T. Ash.* 1–6; *T. Benj.* 4–8). In Christian texts it can be compared with the idea of 'the two ways' expressed in Matthew 7.13-14 and in later Christian literature, such as *Didache* 1–6, *Epistle of Barnabas* 18–21 and Hermas, *Man.* 6.

A transition toward Paul's central belief of justification by divine grace (e.g., Rom. 3.21-31) can be seen, e.g., in 1QS XI.9–15. J. A. Fitzmeyer (1999: 602–605) has shown that, though based on ideas in the Hebrew Bible, the Qumran theology shows a Palestinian Jewish development that has risen to a new plane, having synthesized the ideas of universal sinfulness, dependence on the mercy of a gracious God, and a new state of righteousness derivative from that of God:

> And I belong to the Adam of wickedness and to the assembly of evil flesh. My iniquities, my transgressions, my sins along with the perversities of my heart belong to the assembly of worms and of those who walk in darkness. …to God belongs judgment and from his hands comes perfection of way… But for me, if I falter – the mercies of God are my salvation for ever; and if I stumble in the iniquity of flesh, my judgment is with the righteousness of God, which shall endure for ever… In his compassion he has drawn me near and in his mercies he will bring in my judgment. In the righteousness of his truth he will judge me and in his great goodness he will cover for ever all my iniquities; and in his righteousness he will purify me from the uncleanness of mankind and the sin of the sons of men, that I may praise God for his righteousness and the most high for his majesty. (1QS XI.9–15; trans. A. R. C. Leaney)

Moreover, the idea of mysteries that are revealed only to those chosen by God but hidden from others, which has its prototype in the book of Daniel (e.g, 2.19; 2.28–30, 47), becomes a common theme in Judaism and Christianity. It is used in Matthew and Luke (e.g., Mt. 10.26 = Lk. 12.2; Mt. 11.25 = Lk. 10.21; Mt. 11.27 = Lk. 10.22; Mt. 13.35; Lk. 18.34) and can be compared with that in the Community Rule and other Qumran writings (1QS IV.6; V.11–12; 1QH IX.11; XX.13; 1QpHab VII.4–5; 4Q434 1 i 3–4).

Hebrew and Aramaic Expressions

Some expressions attested in the Community Rule and other Qumran writings provide the Hebrew or Aramaic equivalents of New Testament phrases, documenting that these Hebrew or Aramaic expressions were in use within Judaism during the period when the New Testament writings were being formulated. J.A. Fitzmyer (1998: 614–16) lists, for example, the Pauline expressions 'deeds of the Law' (ἔργα νόμου, Rom. 3.20, 28; Gal. 2.16; 3.2, 5, 10; cf. 4QFlor I.7, 4QMMT C 27; 1QS V.21; VI.18), 'the righteousness of God' (δικαιοσύνη θεοῦ, Rom. 1.17; 3.5, 21, 22.; 10.3; 2 Cor. 5.21) and 'a spirit of holiness' (πνεῦμα ἁγιοσύνης) in parallelism with 'according to the flesh' (κατὰ σάρκα, Rom. 1.3-4; 1QS IV.21; VIII.16; IX.3). Again, just as the Essene community referred to itself as members of 'the Way' (1QS IX.17–18; CD I.13), so too did the early Christian community (Acts 9.2; 19.9, 23; 22.4; 24.14, 22).

Literary Forms

1QS IV.2–14 lists a number of specific behaviours associated with the 'two ways', the way of truth and the way of falsehood, inspired by the Spirit of Truth and the Spirit of Falsehood (cf. Paul's lists 'the fruit of the spirit' and 'the works of the flesh' in Gal. 5.22-23, 19-21). The New Testament contains numerous lists of virtues and vices: Rom. 1.29-31; Gal. 5.16-25; Eph. 4.2-3, 31; 5.3-5; Col. 3.12-14; 1 Tim. 3.2-4; Heb. 7.26; James 3.13; 1 Pet. 2.1; 4.3, 15; Rev. 9.21; 21.8; 22.15. Both the Essene and the Christian lists are influenced by the lists of virtues and vices that were commonplace in contemporary Roman moral philosophy.

Community Structures and Practices

Certain community structures and practices are similar in the Community Rule and the New Testament. (1) At Qumran the term *ha-rabbîm* designates the group of full community members that had judicial functions (e.g. 1QS VI.11–12). This Hebrew word probably lies behind Paul's reference in 2 Cor. 2.5-6 to a punishment by 'the many' (or 'the majority'; cf. also Acts 6.2, 5; 15.12, 30). Again, the eucharistic words 'my blood of the covenant, which is poured out for many' in Mt. 26.27-28 and Mk 14.23-24 may echo the way this term was used at Qumran. Though the designation of 'the many' is somewhat unclear in Matthew and Mark, the parallel in Lk. 22.20, 'poured out for you', shows that Luke understood 'the many' as referring to disciples. Likewise, the Hebrew word for 'the overseer' (*ha-mebaqqer*) is the translational equivalent of *episkopos* ('overseer/bishop') in the New Testament (Phil. 1.1; 1 Tim. 3.1-7; Tit. 1.7-9).

(2) Another feature in common with the Essenes and the followers of Jesus and the early Church is the division into twelve (Jas. 1.1; Mt. 19.28; Lk. 22.30). According to 1QS VIII.1 there should be twelve men and three priests in the council of the community, apparently signifying the twelve tribes of Israel and the three clans of the tribe of Levi (cf. Num. 3.17ff.).

(3) The Community Rule stipulates that all full members were required to share their wealth in common (1QS I.11–13; VI.16–23, 24–25, but cf. CD XIV.11–16). This Essene practice was unusual enough in the Graeco-Roman world to merit

mention by Josephus (*War* II.122), Philo (*Hypoth.* 11.4–9), and Pliny the Elder (*Nat. Hist.* 5.73). Nonetheless, the community's practice shares similarities with the early Christian practice described in Acts 2.44-47; 4.34-37; 5.1-11 (see also Lk. 3.10-14; 8.1-3; 12.33), though in Christianity it was voluntary. The purpose was spiritual, to fulfill the biblical ideas expressed in Lev. 19.18 and Deut. 6.5.

(4) Both the text of the Community Rule and the elaborate system of aqueducts, cisterns, and *miqvaot* in the Qumran compound show that the members practiced ritual immersion in water. This served the practical purpose of purifying the body before the communal meal, but it also symbolized spiritual repentance: 'And it is through the submission of his soul to all the statutes of God that his flesh shall be purified, by being sprinkled with waters for purification and made holy by waters for cleansing' (1QS III.8–9; trans. Knibb). Baptism in the New Testament clearly parallels this practice in general: note John's stress on interior repentance and external good works as the natural expression of repentance (Mk 1.4; Mt. 3.2; Lk. 3.3). There are, however, sharp contrasts. Christian baptism is purely spiritual, not for practical purposes, and it is administered only once, not daily, signifying new birth through Christ's death and resurrection (Harlow 2003: 1581).

(5) The full members of the Essene community shared a common 'pure' meal and drink (1QS VI.16–17, 20–21) in which the priest was to be 'the first to stretch out his hand to bless the first fruits of the bread and the new wine' (1QS VI.4–6). The Rule of the Congregation (1QSa) also describes a ritual for a community meal at which the two Messiahs of Aaron and Israel participate 'at the end of days' (1QSa I.1; II.11–22). This, of course, shares similarities with Jesus' last meal and the Christian eucharist (Mk 14.22-25, Mt. 26.26-29, Lk. 22.17-20; 1 Cor. 11.23-29). Both are ritual meals of a community and mention only bread and wine as constituent elements. Both are implicitly (1QSa I.1–4; cf. CD VI.9; XX.12) or explicitly tied to the 'new covenant' (Mk 14.23-24; 1 Cor. 11.25) and are clearly eschatological and messianic. But a major distinguishing element of the Christian meal is that, in addition to its eschatological character, it is also a memorial: 'Do this in remembrance of me' (1 Cor. 11.25).

(6) The Community Rule proposes a three-stage process for rebuking a fellow community member (1QS V.24–VI.1; see also CD VII.2–3; IX.2–8, 16–20; 4Q477). A similar three-stage process can be seen in Mt. 18.15-17.

Messianism

A broad variety of different hopes that in the Hebrew Bible were barely emerging, grew and developed in the literature of the Essene community. Four different messianic paradigms are detectable in the writings found at Qumran: a king, a priest, a prophet and a heavenly Messiah (Collins 1995). The best-known feature of Qumranic messianism is certainly the idea of a messianic pair formed by the Messiahs of Aaron and Israel.

The passage usually cited as the clearest reference to the two Messiahs can be found in the Community Rule (IX.10–11). The text warns the members of the community against straying from the law of Moses, and stipulates that 'they shall be governed by the first rules in which the men of the community began to be instructed, until the coming of the prophet and the messiahs of Aaron and Israel'. The Hebrew text is unambiguous; the word משיחי is clearly in plural. The two Messiahs are mentioned only in passing, without any further descriptions, and the references to this messianic pair in other Qumran texts are equally opaque (e.g. CD XII.23–XIII.1; XIV.19; XIX.10–11; for the grammatical structure of references in CD, see VanderKam 1994a: 228–31; 1QSa II.18–21).

In the passage of the Community Rule quoted before, a third messianic figure, a prophet, was mentioned. This passage can be compared with another Qumran text entitled Testimonia (4Q175), which is a collection of messianically interpreted biblical quotations. Like the Community Rule, the Testimonia recognizes three messianic figures, for we find side by side a quotation that mentions a prophet like Moses (Exod. 20.18[b] SamPent = Deut. 5.28-29 + 18.18-19 MT), the oracle of Balaam that refers to a kingly Messiah (Num. 24.15-17) and the blessing of Levi, which refers to a priestly Messiah (Deut. 33.8-11). In another Qumran text, 4Q558, the prophet is identified with Elijah, as in the book of Malachi (3.1; 4.5-6).

The similarities and differences between Essene and early Christian messianism have been succinctly summarized by J. VanderKam (1994b: 177–78). He points out that although the texts found at Qumran and the New Testament differ in the question as to how many Messiahs were expected, and who the one arising from the house of David would be, they were similar in assigning a twofold task – kingly and priestly – for the Messiah. Jesus' genealogy going back to David was a sign of his kingly mission. This is clearly reflected in Acts 2.29-31 as Peter speaks on Pentecost: 'our ancestor David … Since he was a prophet, he knew that God had sworn an oath to him that he would put one of his descendants on his throne. Foreseeing this, David spoke of the resurrection of the Messiah.' Jesus' priestly mission is emphasized in the Letter to the Hebrews: Jesus is the priest according to order of Melchizedek, and he performs his high priestly duty in a heavenly temple (cf. 11QMelchizedek). Both the priestly and the kingly aspects of Jesus' work are reflected upon in Heb. 10.12–13: 'when Christ had offered for all time a single sacrifice for sins, "he sat down at the right hand of God," and since then has been waiting "until his enemies would be made a footstool for his feet"'. Thus, the Essenes awaited two Messiahs, one kingly, and one priestly, whereas the early Christians acknowledged only one Messiah, in which the two aspects of his work were combined.

Further Reading

Bauckham, R., 'The Qumran Community and the Gospel of John', in L. H. Schiffman, E. Tov and J. C. VanderKam (eds), *The Dead Sea Scrolls: Fifty Years after Their Discovery 1947–1997: Proceedings of the Jerusalem Congress, July 20–25, 1997* (Jerusalem: Israel Exploration Society in cooperation with the Shrine of the Book Museum, Israel, 2000), pp. 105–15.

Brooke, G. J., 'Isaiah 40:3 and the Wilderness Community', in G. J. Brooke and F. García Martínez (eds), *New Qumran Texts and Studies: Proceedings of the First Meeting of the International Organization for Qumran Studies, Paris 1992* (Leiden: Brill, 1994), pp. 117–32.

Charlesworth, J. H., 'Intertextuality: Isaiah 40:3 and the Serek ha-Yaḥad,' in C. A. Evans and S. Talmon (eds), *The Quest for Context and Meaning: Studies in Biblical Intertextuality in Honor of James A. Sanders* (Biblical Interpretation Series, 28; Leiden: Brill, 1997), pp. 197–224.

Collins, J. J., *The Scepter and the Star: The Messiahs of the Dead Sea Scrolls and Other Ancient Literature* (New York: Doubleday, 1995).

Cross, F. M., *The Ancient Library of Qumran* (Minneapolis: Fortress Press, 3rd edn, 1995), esp. pp. 143–70.

Evans, C. A. and P. W. Flint, *Eschatology, Messianism, and the Dead Sea Scrolls* (Studies in the Dead Sea Scrolls and Related Literature, 1; Grand Rapids, MI and Cambridge: Eerdmans, 1997).

Fitzmyer, J. A., 'The Use of Explicit Old Testament Quotations in Qumran Literature and in the New Testament', *NTS* 7 (1961), pp. 297–333.

—'Paul and the Dead Sea Scrolls', in P. W. Flint and J. C. VanderKam (eds), *The Dead Sea Scrolls After Fifty Years: A Comprehensive Assessment*, vol. 2 (Leiden: Brill, 1998), pp. 599–621.

—*The Dead Sea Scrolls and Christian Origins* (Studies in the Dead Sea Scrolls and Related Literature; Grand Rapids, MI: Eerdmans, 2000).

Fraade, S. D., 'Interpretive Authority in the Studying Community at Qumran', *JJS* 44 (1993), pp. 46–69.

—'Looking for Legal Midrash at Qumran', in M. E. Stone and E. G. Chazon (eds), *Biblical Perspectives: Early Use and Interpretation of the Bible in Light of the Dead Sea Scrolls* (STDJ, 28; Leiden: Brill, 1998), pp. 59–79.

Harlow, D. C., 'The Dead Sea Scrolls and the New Testament', in J. C. Dunn and J. W. Rogerson (eds), *Eerdmans Commentary on the Bible* (Grand Rapids, MI: Eerdmans, 2003), pp. 1577–86.

Hempel, C. 'Interpretative Authority in the Community Rule Tradition', *DSD* 10 (2003), pp. 59–80.

Knibb, M., 'Eschatology and Messianism in the Dead Sea Scrolls', in P. W. Flint and J. C. VanderKam (eds), *The Dead Sea Scrolls After Fifty Years: A Comprehensive Assessment*, vol. 2 (Leiden: Brill, 1999), pp. 379–402.

Metso, S., 'Biblical Quotations in the Community Rule', in E. D. Herbert and E. Tov (eds); *The Bible as Book: The Hebrew Bible and the Judaean Desert Discoveries* (London: The British Library and Oak Knoll Press in association with The Scriptorium: Center for Christian Antiquities, 2002), pp. 81–92.

Murphy, C. M., *Wealth in the Dead Sea Scrolls and in the Qumran Community* (Leiden: Brill, 2001).

—*John the Baptist: Prophet of Purity for a New Age* (Collegeville, MN: Liturgical Press, 2003).

Taylor, J., 'The Community of Goods among the First Christians and among the Essenes', in D. Goodblatt, A. Pinnick and D. R. Schwartz (eds), *Historical Perspectives: From the Hasmoneans to Bar Kokhba in Light of the Dead Sea Scrolls. Proceedings of the Fourth International Symposium of the Orion Center for the Study of the Dead Sea Scrolls and Associated Literature, 27–31 January 1999* (STDJ, 37; Leiden: Brill, 2001), pp. 147–61.

Taylor, J. E., *The Immerser: John the Baptist within Second Temple Judaism* (Grand Rapids, MI: Eerdmans, 1997).

VanderKam, J. C., 'Messianism in the Scrolls', in E. Ulrich and J. VanderKam (eds), *The Community of the Renewed Covenant* (Notre Dame, IN: University of Notre Dame Press, 1994), pp. 211–34.

—*The Dead Sea Scrolls Today* (Grand Rapids, MI: Eerdmans, 1994), esp. pp. 159–85.

Vermes, G., 'Biblical Proof-Texts in Qumran Literature', *JSS* 34 (1989), pp. 493–508.
—'The Qumran Community, the Essenes and Nascent Christianity', in L. H. Schiffman, E. Tov and J. C. VanderKam, *The Dead Sea Scrolls Fifty Years After Their Discovery* (Jerusalem: Israel Exploration Society/Shrine of the Book Museum, Israel, 2000), pp. 581–86.
Wernberg-Møller, P., 'Some Reflections on the Biblical Material in the Manual of Discipline', *ST* 9 (1955), pp. 40–66.

Chapter 6

TEXTS RELATED TO THE COMMUNITY RULE

Rule of the Congregation (1QSa)

The Rule of the Congregation has often been described as an appendix to 1QS. The fact that the first copy found was physically stitched to 1QS, as well as the siglum assigned to it (1QSa) reflect that idea. The other nine manuscripts subsequently found from Cave 4 and identified by S. Pfann (2000) as representing this document, however, attest to its independence. The nine copies are all extremely fragmentary and all written on papyrus in the cryptic script. But irrespective of the size of the fragments, none contain material from the *Serekh*, and it is clear that the Rule of the Congregation should be understood on its own terms rather than through its physical link to 1QS. Indeed, the Cave 4 copies of this text bear the more suitable siglum 4QSE, the initials SE referring to the title *Serekh ha-'Edah* (סרך העדה) that stands at the beginning of the document.

The Rule of the Congregation poses a challenge to its interpreters. In terms of its genre, it can be compared to other rule texts found at Qumran, but in most compendia of DSS translations, the document is classified as an 'eschatological work', and sometimes called a 'Messianic Rule'. This reflects the view of many commentators that the Rule of the Congregation describes a future, eschatological community. Nevertheless, the document mirrors many rules of everyday practice in the Damascus Document and the Community Rule, and while the document does have an eschatological perspective especially in its concluding section, it is important to realize that 'the end of days' (אחרית הימים) referred to in the opening words of the document ('This is the rule for the whole congregation of Israel at the end of days', 1QSa I.1) was the time period in which the community thought it was already living (Steudel 1992: 225–46). That is, the period they termed 'the end of days' had already begun, although its culmination, the coming of the Messiahs, had not yet happened.

Another challenge for interpreters has been the question of the identity of the group behind this document. L. Schiffman (1989: 69), speaking of 1QSa as the messianic mirror of the actual life in the Qumran community, indicates the groups behind these texts to have been identical. P. Davies (1994: 59–60), on the other hand, has argued that the group described in this text is different from both of those behind the Community Rule and the Damascus Document. C. Hempel (1996) thinks that 1QSa has preserved in its nucleus a corpus of ancient community legislation, going back to the parent movement of the *yaḥad* group. Yet another view is that by H. Stegemann (1998: 113–15), who does not see the rule as eschato-logical, but considers it the oldest of the rules of the Essene community.

1QSa I.1–5: Introduction
The text is addressed to 'the whole congregation of Israel', but it is unlikely that the intention of this address would have been to embrace those outside the commu-nity. Rather, in the community's view, 'at the end of days' its members, and only they, would be identified with the true Israel, as the elect of God; and its enemies, those who '[walk in t]he way of the people', would eventually be destroyed (cf. War Scroll). The authority in the congregation is given to the Zadokite priests and their followers, who are portrayed as keepers of the covenant. Remarkably, in this covenant women and children are included, and they shall be present when the statutes of the covenant are publicly read.

1QSa I.6–25a: Education and Official Duties in the Congregation
The initiation into the community and its rules starts at an early age and continues until the age of 20, when full membership is granted with the recognition that the member is now fully capable of moral discernment and has reached the age of marriageability. Certain congregational and military duties, however, especially those involving leadership positions, are not accessible until later. Those deemed simpletons are excluded from congregational and military service except for menial labor. A strict hierarchy prevails in the congregation under the leadership of the Zadokite priests, the heads of the families and the Levites.

1QSa I.25b–II.11a: Assemblies of the Congregation
Access to meetings where judicial decrees were issued and other matters of high-est importance, such as mobilization for war, were decided upon, was highly restricted. A three-day period of ritual sanctification was required (cf. Exod. 19.10-11), and only those whose conduct was perfect and who were physically unblemished were allowed to attend. The ritual purity of the assembly had to be guarded, and any impurity, whether physical or mental, had to be eliminated. In the sacred realm that was thus created, holy angels were present (cf. 1QM VII.6; 1QS XI.8).

1QSa II.11b–17a: Order in the Messianic Council
The eschatological nature of the document is most evident in its last two sections that presume two messianic figures, one priestly, the other kingly, at the head of the council of the community and the common meal. It is unfortunate that the manuscript is quite fragmentary in this part. In the session of the messianic coun-cil, strict hierarchical order is again followed: the priestly Messiah with the accom-panying priests, i.e. the sons of Aaron, comprise the first rank, the kingly Messiah is next along with the accompanying heads of the clans of Israel. The third group is formed by the heads of families and the wise men of the congregation.

1QSa II.17b–22: The Messianic Banquet

This meal of bread and wine is often compared with the Christian eucharistic meal (Mk 14.22-25 par.; in *eschaton* Mt. 22.1-12, Rev. 19.6-21), but the theme of the eschatological banquet is deeply rooted in the Jewish tradition (see, e.g., Isa. 25.6-8; Joel 2.24-28; *1 En.* 62.12-14; *2 Bar.* 29). The two Messiahs preside over this meal and are the first to bless the bread and wine before the other participants. The concluding statement of the passage shows that the common meals of the community somehow anticipated this messianic event (see also 1QS VI.3–5), but what the exact character of these communal meals was, for example, whether they should be understood as 'sacral' meals or they were in some other sense 'pure' meals (see 1QS VI.16–17, 20), continues to be disputed (Schiffman 1989: 59–64).

The literary style employed in the document is rich with allusions to phrases and expressions of the Hebrew Bible, particularly in the priestly layers of the Pentateuch (for parallels see Knibb 1987: 145–55; Schiffman 1989; Charlesworth and Stuckenbruck 1994a: 109). The language and imagery used of the community reflects biblical exodus and wilderness traditions. This is evident already in the introduction to the document that addresses the community as the 'whole congregation of Israel' (cf., e.g., Exod. 12.3, 6, 19; 16.1; 35.1), but even more so in the way the community is organized in the manner of a military camp (1QSa I.14–15; II.15; cf. Exod. 18.21; Deut. 1.15; Num. 10.11-18). Israel's direct and close relationship with God and faithfulness to his commands during that period served as the ultimate model applicable even for the messianic age (Schiffman 1989: 70)

Within the Qumran corpus, the Rule of the Congregation has connections especially with the War Scroll, the Damascus Document, and the Community Rule. To mention a few examples, the age limits set for official duties in 1QSa I.13–23 can be compared with similar regulations in 1QM VI.13–VII.3 and CD X.6–10 and XIV.6–10, and the exclusion of the physically and mentally disabled in 1QSa II.3–11 is also mentioned in 1QM VII.4–6 and CD XV.15–17. The strict hierarchy of the community assemblies in 1QSa II.12–17 can be compared with 1QS VI.8–13; the description of the meal in 1QSa II.17–22 can be compared with 1QS VI.4–6; and the references to the sons of Zadok in 1QSa I. 2, 24, and II.3 have parallels in 1QS V.2, 9 (cf., however, 4QS[b,d]).

The Rule of the Congregation is one of the Qumran scrolls that contain references to women and children. According to 1QSa I.4 women and children are present when 'the statutes of the covenant' are read aloud. Much attention has also been given to a possible reference to the testimony of women in judicial proceedings in 1QS I.11, but the context indicates that the text has a grammatical error and should be amended to refer to a male community member instead (Baumgarten 1977b: 183–86). Moreover, the Rule of the Congregation illuminates the upbringing of children. Rabbinic texts provide interesting parallels to the education of children and the different stages of life. Mishnah 'Abot 5.21, for example, similarly describes stages of gradual initiation into the observance of religious rules, and into the growing responsibilities of a member of a religious community and of a married life. The minimum age of 20 for public officials is attested in many rabbinic sources (e.g. *t. Hag.* 1.3; *b. Hul.* 24b; *y. San.* 4.7); the biblical basis for the minimum age of 20 is most likely in the rules of census, see Exod. 30.14 and 38.26 (Schiffman 1983: 58–60).

For New Testament studies, the Rule of the Congregation is particularly significant in its description of the messianic figures and of the common meal. Although the significance of the communal meals of the Essene community clearly differed from the eucharistic meals of the early Christians, they can be compared insofar as 'both meals feature bread and wine, both are eschatological and messianic in character, and both have an anticipatory element' (Harlow 2003, 1581).

Editions and Further Reading

Barthélemy, D., '1Q28a. Règle de la Congrégation (1QSa)', in D. Barthélemy and J. T. Milik, *Qumran Cave I* (DJD, 1; Oxford: Clarendon Press, 1955), pp. 107–18, pls. XXII–XXIV.

Baumgarten, J. M., 'On the Testimony of Women in 1QSa', in *Studies in Qumran Law* (STDJ, 24; Leiden: Brill, 1977), pp. 183–86 [= *JBL* 76 (1957), pp. 266–69].

Carmignac, J., 'La Règle de la congrégation', in J. Carmignac, É. Cothenet and H. Lignée (eds), *Les Textes de Qumrân*, vol. 2 (Paris: Letouzet et Ané, 1963), pp. 10–27.

—'Quelques détails de lecture dans la "Règle de la congregation", le "Recueil des benedictions", et les "Dires de Moïse"', *RevQ* 13 (1963), pp. 83–96.

Charlesworth, J. H., and L. T. Stuckenbruck, 'Rule of the Congregation (1QSa)', in J. H. Charlesworth *et al.* (eds) *The Dead Sea Scrolls: Hebrew, Aramaic, and Greek Texts with English Translations*, vol. 1: *Rule of the Community and Related Documents* (Tübingen: J. C. B. Mohr [Paul Siebeck]; Louisville, KY: Westminster John Knox Press, 1994), pp. 108–17.

Cross, F. M., 'Qumran Cave I', *JBL* 75 (1956), pp. 121–25.

Davies, P. R., 'Communities in the Qumran Scrolls', *Proceedings of the Irish Biblical Association* 17 (1994), pp. 55–68.

Hempel, C. 'The Early Essene Nucleus of 1QSa', *DSD* 3 (1996), pp. 253–69.

Knibb, M. A., *The Qumran Community* (Cambridge Commentaries on Writings of the Jewish and Christian World 200 BC to AD 200, 2; Cambridge: Cambridge University Press, 1987), pp. 145–55.

Pfann, S. J., '4Q249a-i: 4QpapCryptA Serekh ha-'Edah[a-j]', in *Qumran Cave 4.XXVI: Cryptic Texts* (DJD, 36; Oxford: Clarendon Press, 2000), pp. 515–74, pls. XXXV-XXXVII.

Schiffman, L. H., *Sectarian Law in the Dead Sea Scrolls: Courts, Testimony and the Penal Code* (BJS, 33; Chico, CA: Scholars Press, 1983).

—*The Eschatological Community of the Dead Sea Scrolls: A Study of the Rule of the Congregation* (Atlanta: Scholars Press, 1989).

Stegemann, H., *The Library of Qumran: On the Essenes, Qumran, John the Baptist, and Jesus* (orig. *Die Essener, Qumran, Johannes der Täufer und Jesus: Ein Sachbuch* [Freiburg: Herder, 1993]; Grand Rapids, MI: Eerdmans; Leiden: Brill, 1998), pp. 113–15.

Steudel, A., 'אחרית הימים' in the Texts from Qumran', *RevQ* 16 (1992), pp. 225–46.

Yadin, Y., 'A Crucial Passage in the Dead Sea Scrolls: 1QSa ii.11–17', *JBL* (1959), pp. 238–41.

Rule of the Blessings (1QSb)

The third manuscript copied in the same scroll with 1QS and 1QSa is somewhat misleadingly often entitled Rule of the Blessings, for in terms of its genre it is not a rule but rather a liturgical text comparable, for example, to 4QBerakhot and 4QDaily Blessings. The content of the manuscript forms a series of blessings pronounced over various groups and individuals; preserved as addressees are 'those who fear God' (i.e., the congregation), Zadokite priests (possibly including a priestly messiah or a high priest), and the prince of the congregation, i.e. the kingly messiah. Parts of five columns are preserved, but they are all very fragmentary, and considerable disagreement prevails regarding the overall structure of the text and the identity of persons or groups to be blessed (Milik 1955: 118–30; Licht 1965: 273–89; Schiffman 1989: 72–76, Charlesworth and Stuckenbruck 1994b: 119–31). For our discussion, the manuscript is relevant in regard to terminological overlaps with S and Sa, and will be discussed here only briefly.

The title of the work and subheadings (1QSb I.1; III.22; V.20) address the manuscript to the wise leader, that is, the *maskîl*, the community official mentioned also in the Rule of the Community, whose duties appear to have been more spiritual than administrative in nature (1QS III.13; 4QS^b IX.1 // 4QS^d I.1; 1QS IX.12,21). The manuscript also mentions the 'sons of Zadok' (1QSb III.22), a term shared with both the Community Rule and the Rule of the Congregation (1QS V.2, 9; 1QSa I.24; II.3), the *rabbîm* (1QSb IV.27), that is, the general council of the community (cf. 1QS VI.8), and the *yaḥad* (1QSb V.21), that is, the community (1QS I.1; V.1); thus, the manuscript clearly is a product of an Essene community.

The blessings in 1QSb can be compared with the blessings of the covenant ceremony in 1QS I–II (esp. II.1–4), but conspicuously, no curses are included in 1QSb, indicating that the documents was intended for the messianic age, when the final victory over the forces of darkness would have already been achieved. The text may alternatively have been meant for use in a ceremony anticipating the messianic age. As in the Rule of the Congregation, the presence of heavenly beings (see 'angel of presence' in 1QSb IV.25, 26) is assumed, as the prince of the congregation and those chosen for 'the eternal covenant' gather.

Editions and Further Reading

Abegg, M. G., Jr, '1QSb and the Elusive High Priest', in S. M. Paul, R. A. Kraft, L. H. Schiffman and W. W. Fields (eds), *Emanuel: Studies in Hebrew Bible, Septuagint, and Dead Sea Scrolls in Honor of Emanuel Tov* (VTSup, 94; Leiden: Brill, 2003), pp. 3–16.

Brooke, G. J., 'Appendix. 1Q28b. 1QSerekh ha-Yaḥad b (fragment)', in P. S. Alexander and G. Vermes, *Qumran Cave 4.XIX: Serekh ha-Yaḥad and Two Related Texts* (DJD, 26; Oxford: Clarendon Press, 1998), pp. 227–33.

Carmignac, J., 'Le Recueil des bénédictions', in J. Carmignac, É. Cothenet and H. Lignée (eds), *Les Textes de Qumrân*, vol. 2 (Paris: Letouzet et Ané, 1963), pp. 28–42.

—'Quelques détails de lecture dans la "Règle de la congregation", le "Recueil des benedictions", et les "Dires de Moïse"', *RevQ* 13 (1963), pp. 83–96.

Charlesworth, J. H. and L. T. Stuckenbruck, 'Blessings', in J. H. Charlesworth *et al.* (eds), *The Dead Sea Scrolls: Hebrew, Aramaic, and Greek Texts with English Translations*, vol. 1: *Rule of the Community and Related Documents* (Tübingen: J. C. B. Mohr [Paul Siebeck]; Louisville, KY: Westminster John Knox Press, 1994), pp. 119–31.

Licht, J., *Megillat has-Serakim: The Rule Scroll: A Scroll from the Wilderness of Judaea: 1QS, 1QSa, 1QSb: Text, Introduction and Commentary* (Jerusalem: Mosad Bialik, 1965), pp. 273–89.

Milik, J. T., 'Recueil des Bénédictions (1QSb)', in D. Barthélemy and J. T. Milik (eds), *Qumran Cave I* (DJD, 1; Oxford: Clarendon, 1955), pp. 118–30, plates XXV–XXIX.

Schiffman, L. H., *The Eschatological Community of the Dead Sea Scrolls: A Study of the Rule of the Congregation* (SBLMS, 38; Atlanta: Scholars Press, 1989), pp. 72–76.

Talmon, S., 'The "Manual of Benedictions" of the Sect of the Judaean Desert', *RevQ* 8 (1960), pp. 475–500.

Miscellaneous Rules (4Q265; formerly Serekh Dameseq)

Among the rule texts found at Qumran, 4Q265 proves to be an interesting case. Though only seven of the nineteen fragments of this manuscript are large enough for content analysis, a veritable gamut of topics and literary genres emerges, including biblical proof-texts from prophetic books, penal regulations, rules for admission into the community, Sabbath halakah, a description of the council of the community (עצת היחד), rules for childbirth, and a paraphrase of the Adam and Eve narrative. Thus, like the Damascus Document, 4Q265 mentions women and children and includes rules that are typical for the Damascus Document (e.g. Sabbath regulations), while the organizational terminology of the manuscript, most notably the mention of the council of the community, connects it with the Community Rule. This combination of features from both S and D traditions was emphasized in the former name of the manuscript, *Serekh Dameseq*, but as noted by J. Baumgarten (1999: 58), the editor of 4Q265, the name Miscellaneous Rules more accurately reflects the diverse contents of this manuscript.

For our interest in the connections between the Community Rule and 4Q265, four features of this manuscript deserve to be highlighted: the nature of the penal code, the use of biblical proof-texts, the organizational terminology, and rules for admission into the community. A fuller discussion of this manuscript has appeared in C. Hempel's volume 'The Damascus Texts' in this same series 'Companion to the Qumran Scrolls' (2000).

The penal code of 4Q265 lists transgressions which occur in the Community Rule and in the Cave 4 fragments of the Damascus Document, such as complaining against those ranked higher in the community (1QS VI.25–27 // 4Q265 frg. 4 i 6–7), lying (1QS VII.3–4 // 4Q265 frg. 4 i 10–11), insulting a neighbour (1QS VII.8 // 4Q265 frg. 4 i 8 // 4QD[a] 10 ii.2–3) or betraying a neighbour (1QS VII.5 // 4Q265 frg. 4 i 9–10), falling asleep in the community meeting (1QS VII.10 // 4Q265 frg. 4 i 12 – ii 1 // 4QD[a] 10 ii.5–6) and guffawing stupidly (1QS VII.14–15 // 4Q265 frg. 4 i 4 // 4QD[e] 7 i.4). Whereas the Community Rule always lists a single punishment, a double punishment consisting of fine and exclusion occurs in 4Q265; this feature connects it with Cave 4 manuscripts of the Damascus Document, 4Q266 (4QD[a]) and 4Q270 (4QD[e]). Interestingly, the length of the exclusion in 4Q265 and 4QD corresponds to the length of the fine in 1QS. Whereas in the Community Rule and the Damascus Document the exact nature of the fine is in many cases unclear, 4Q265 explicitly states that the fine signifies cutting the food ration. Only once in 1QS is cutting the food ration mentioned (VI.25). The parallel of this case in 4Q265 lists a punishment more severe than the one in 1QS.

Another interesting feature of 4Q265 is its use of Hebrew Bible quotations. Baumgarten notes that here 4Q265 resembles 4QOrdinances, for both of them 'embrace biblical quotations and narrative allusions which are not strictly halakhic, but may have served as support for rules propounded by Qumran exegetes' (1999: 60) The use of biblical proof-texts is also attested in 1QS and CD; even the same introductory formulas כאשר כתוב בספר / כאשר כתוב which occur in 1QS and CD, occur also in fragment 1 of 4Q265 (cf. 4Q265 frg. 1 lines 2 and 3; 1QS V.17; VIII.14; CD VII.10,19). The text in 4Q265 has preserved quotes from Isa. 54.1-2 (frg. 1) and Mal. 2.10 (frg. 3), and a paraphrase of Lev. 12.1-4. The context of the first quote, Isa. 54.1-2, is not preserved. The second one, Mal. 2.10, appears to have been used to provide justification for the exclusion of women and minors from the partaking of the paschal sacrifices. The third one, paraphrased Lev. 12.1-4, gives a basis for the purification rules of childbirth. Like 4Q265, the Community Rule uses quotes from both prophetic (Isa. 2.22 in 1QS V.16–19; Isa. 40.3 in 1QS VIII.12–16) and Pentateuchal (Exod. 23.7 in 1QS V.13–16) books.

The organizational terminology used in 4Q265 clearly identifies the text as Essene, but the exact sociological outlook of the community behind 4Q265 is difficult to determine: the terms *rabbîm* (4Q265 frg. 4 ii.4 and 5) and 'the man at the head of the *rabbîm*' (4Q265 frg. 4 ii.8) are attested in both S and D, whereas 'session of the *rabbîm*' (4Q265 frg. 4 ii.1) and 'council of the community' (4Q265 frg. 7, lines 7 and 8) are used only in S manuscripts and not in D. Particularly interesting is the passage in 4Q265 frg. 7 lines 7–11 that has significant overlaps with 1QS VIII.1–10. Both passages start with the formulaic בהיות and speak of a group of fifteen men in the community council (בעצת היחד). In 1QS, the group of fifteen is said to consist of twelve men and three priests (שנים עשר איש וכוהנים של ושה). 4Q265, although the text is fragmentary at this point, appears to state only the number fifteen without distinction of roles. Both passages state that the council of community is 'established in truth' (נכונה העצת היחד באמת) and that the members of the council are 'chosen by the will of God' (בחירי רצון). Both passages compare the council to the 'aroma of a pleasing fragrance' (ריח ניחוח) and state that the purpose of the council is to 'bring atonement to the land' (לכפר על/בעד הארץ) and that there will be an end to 'injustice' (עולה). Obviously, there is a literary dependency, direct or indirect, between these passages. Baumgarten (1999: 58) designates the council mentioned in 4Q265 as an 'Eschatological Communal Council' apparently on the basis of frg. 7 line 10: 'the periods of iniquity will come to an end by judgment'. In the light of the similar statement in 1QS VIII.10, however, an eschatological interpretation may not be required.

Another passage of interest is in 4Q265 4 ii 3–9 where the rules of admission into the community, identified with the 'council of the community', are recounted. The passage is preserved only very fragmentarily, but 4Q265 appears to have envisioned a lengthy procedure consisting of several stages like the procedure described in 1QS VI.13–23, as opposed to a shorter procedure recorded in CD XV.5–10 and 1QS V.7–11.

Edition and Further Reading

Baumgarten, J., 'The Cave 4 Versions of the Qumran Penal Code', *JJS* 43 (1992), pp. 268–76.
—'Scripture and Law in 4Q265', in M. E. Stone and E. G. Chazon (eds), *Biblical Perspectives: Early Use and Interpretation of the Bible in Light of the Dead Sea Scrolls* (STDJ, 28; Leiden: Brill, 1998), pp. 25–33.
—'4QMiscellaneous Rules (4Q265), ' in J. Baumgarten *et al.*, *Qumran Cave 4.XXV: Halakhic Texts* (DJD, 35; Oxford: Clarendon Press, 1999), pp. 57–78, pls V-VII.
Hempel, C., *The Damascus Texts* (Companion to the Qumran Scrolls, 1; Sheffield: Sheffield Academic Press 2000), esp. pp. 89–104.
Milik, J. T., *Ten Years of Discovery in the Wilderness of Judaea* (trans. J. Strugnell [*Dix ans de découvertes dans le Désert de Juda*; Paris: Cerf, 1957]; SBT, 26; London 1959), p. 90.

Rebukes Reported by the Overseer (4Q477; formerly Decrees)

This manuscript with only five remaining fragments provides an intimate glimpse of community life: members mentioned by name are rebuked for moral offenses, such as being short-tempered, haughty in spirit or disturbing the spirit of the community. Apparently, the fragments belong to a legal list of members who had sinned and therefore been rebuked as the first step of the community's judicial process. The body of the text is formulaic, following the pattern: 'And they rebuke X son of Y' + allusion to the man's sin; e.g., 'And Hananiah Notos was rebuked because he [... to dis]turb the spirit of the Yaḥad ...'. Although the text is not explicit as to who carried out the rebuke (Hempel 1995; Reed 1996), E. Eshel, the editor of the text, finds it likely that the rebukes were recorded by the *mebaqqer*, the overseer, since he is mentioned in CD ms. A IX.16–20 as the one officiating at the process (2000: 474–75).

The rule of rebuke is based on Lev. 19.17: 'You shall not hate in your heart anyone of your kin; you shall reprove your neighbor, or you will incur guilt yourself' (NRSV). In addition to the Dead Sea Scrolls, references to the practice of rebuke are found in Sir. 19.13-17, *T. Gad.* 6.1-5, and Mt. 18.15-17a, attesting that the practice of rebuke was widespread in Second Temple times. The practice is referred to in CD IX.2–4:

> And what he said: *Lev 19:18* 'Do not avenge yourself or bear resentment against the sons of your people': everyone of those brought to the covenant who brings an accusation against his fellow, unless it is with reproach before witnesses, or brings it when he is angry, or tells it to his elders so that they might despise him, he is 'the one who avenges himself and bears resentment' (CD IX.2–4; trans. García-Martínez and Tigchelaar).

It is also discussed in 1QS V.24–VI.1:

> They shall reprove one another *in tr[uth]*, *humility*, and kindly love *towards man*. Let no man speak to his neighbour in anger or in complaint or *with a [stiff] neck [or* in a jealou]s *spirit of* wickedness, *and let him not hate him [...] of his heart. But let him reprove him on the same day lest he incur guilt because of him.* And let no man bring a matter against his neighbour before the rabbim except after reproof before witnesses. (1QS V.24–VI.1; trans. Knibb, modified by Metso; text in italics not included in 4QS^d).

Both D and S indicate that rebuke was to be carried out before bringing the case to the elders (CD) or the *rabbîm* (1QS). In light of the passage in CD IX.2–4, the penal regulation in 1QS VII.8–9 should probably be understood as referring to those who had failed to follow the rule of reproof and were therefore punished: 'Whoever bears a grudge against his neighbour without cause shall be fined for six months{one year}. And likewise for anyone who avenges anything himself.' Thus, as an initial step the practice of reproof appears to have been an important part of the community's judicial process.

In regard to organizational terminology, 4Q477 is similar to 4Q265 in that it combines terms from both S and D traditions. That is, individual terms once thought to belong uniquely either to S or to D traditions are found in combination in 4Q477, as they are in 4Q265. Most significantly, 4Q477 frg. 2 i.3 refers to 'the camp of the *rabbim*' (מחני הרבים). The term מחנה does not occur in S at all, whereas it is very common in D; the term הרבים is used both in S and D, but the combination מחני הרבים is attested in 4Q477 only.

Edition and Further Reading

Eshel, E., '4QRebukes Reported by the Overseer', in *Qumran Cave 4.XXVI: Cryptic Texts and Miscellanea, part 1* (DJD, 36; Oxford: Clarendon Press, 2000]), pp. 474–83 and pl. XXXII.

Hempel, C., 'Who Rebukes in *4Q477*?', *RevQ* 16 (1995), pp. 655–56.

Nitzan, B., 'The Laws of Reproof in 4QBerakhot (4Q286–290) in Light of their Parallels in the Damascus Covenant and other Texts from Qumran', in M. Bernstein, F. García Martínez and J. Campen (eds.), *Legal Texts and Legal Issues: Proceedings of the Second Meeting of the International Organization for Qumran Studies, Cambridge 1995* (STDJ, 23; Leiden: Brill, 1997), pp. 149–65.

Reed, S., 'Genre, Setting, and Title of 4Q477', *JJS* 47 (1996), pp. 147–48.

Communal Ceremony (4Q275)

The manuscript 4Q275 has preserved some wording similar to that of 1QS I–IV, especially to the liturgy of the renewal of the covenant (1QS II.18–III.12). Despite the similar wording, the remains of the manuscript are so small that it is difficult to establish the contents, genre, or structure of the full composition. Judging from the three small fragments preserved, part of it seems to present a covenant-renewal liturgy. Two clues in particular point on that direction. Firstly, the date בחודש השלישי] ('in the third month'; frg. 1 line 3). A gathering of the members in the third month is mentioned in the Damascus Document manuscript 4Q270 (4QD^e) frg. 7 II.11, and this presumably refers to the renewal of the covenant. Secondly, the text speaks about registering a member, testing and rebuking him; and blessings and curses were apparently also included. The liturgy in the Community Rule implies that the new members were accepted during the renewal of the covenant. Another connection with the Community Rule is the use of the term נחלה ('inheritance') that is mentioned twice in 4Q275. In the Community Rule it is used in the sense that everyone is assigned a lot under the dominion of either the Prince of Light or the Prince of Darkness (1QS IV.15–16, 24). Moreover, the text mentions organizational functionaries similar to the ones in the Community Rule and the Damascus Document: the elders (הזקנים) and the *mebaqqer* (המבקר). The members are also referred to by the name קרי השם ('the called ones of name') which has a parallel in CD IV.3–4 בחירי ישראל קריאי השם ('the chosen ones of Israel, the called ones of name').

Edition and Further Reading

Alexander, P. S., and G. Vermes, '4QCommunal Ceremony (4Q275)', in P. S. Alexander and
    G. Vermes, *Qumran Cave 4.XIX: 4QSerekh Ha-Yaḥad and Two Related Texts* (DJD, 26;
    Oxford: Clarendon Press, 1998), pp. 209–16.
Metso, S., 'Constitutional Rules at Qumran', in P. W. Flint and J. C.VanderKam (eds), *The
    Dead Sea Scrolls After Fifty Years. A Comprehensive Assessment*, vol. 1 (Leiden: Brill,
    1998), pp. 186–210 (esp. 205–207).
Milik, J. T., 'Milkî-ṣedeq et Milkî-resa' dans les anciens écrits juifs et chrétiens', *JJS* 23
    (1972), pp. 95–144 (esp. pp. 129–30).

Four Lots (4Q279)

Only one of the five remaining fragments of 4Q279 is large enough for an attempt at content analysis of this manuscript, and despite relative certainty of transcription, the preserved words are open to interpretation. What seems to be clear is that frg. 5 speaks of groups of community members and hierarchical order, for the ordinal number 'fourth' is preserved, and of the four ranked groups of the community that presumably were listed two remain, namely 'priests, the sons of Aaron' (כה]נים בני אהרון) and 'proselytes' (גר]ים). Similar rules with an emphasis on the hierarchical order of different groups of the community are included e.g. in CD XIV.3–6 and 1QS II.19–25 and VI.8–9. The passage in CD XIV.3–6 may provide the closest parallel for the list of community members, for like 4Q279, it speaks of inscribing (כתב) the order of the members: 'Rule of the session of all the camps. All shall be enlisted by their names: the priests first, the levites second, the children of Israel third, and the proselytes fourth; and they shall be inscribed by their [na]mes, each one after his brother; the priests first, the levites second, the children of Israel third and the proselytes fourth'. Perhaps the text of 4Q279 should be reconstructed accordingly so that the four groups discussed would be 'priests the son of Aaron, Levites, children of Israel, and proselytes' (כוהנים בני אהרון, לויים, בני ישראל, and גרים).

Significant for the understanding of the nature and purpose of this document is the word הגורל, 'lot', that occurs three times in frg. 5, once in the wording יצא הגור]ל, 'to cast lot'. This term is used in the Community Rule particularly in the treatise on the two spirits to denote the two opposing 'lots' of God and Belial, or the lots of the Spirit of Truth and of Injustice (1QS III.24; IV.24, 26), but also to denote the 'lot' or predestined position of an individual within either of these camps (1QS I.10; II.2, 5, 17). The wording יצא הגור]ל 'to cast lot' belongs to the context of communal decision-making, particularly of the *rabbîm* as they, for example, made decisions about the new members to be admitted into the community (1QS V.3; VI.16 ,18, 22; IX.7). In this context, the wording יצא הגורל 'to cast lot' should probably understood figuratively rather than literally. A similar wording הפיל הגורל 'cast lot, lit. to cause the lot to fall' is used in in the Rule of the Blessings (1QSb IV.26) and the treatise on the two spirits (1QSb IV.26) in eschatological contexts, and in the War Rule (1QM I.12–15) the term גורל is used to denote a phase in the eschatological battle. Perhaps because of these connections the editors of 4Q279, P. Alexander and G. Vermes, 'very tentatively suggest that 4Q279 is the remains of a Messianic Rule' (1998: 218). A messianic interpretation may not be necessary, however, especially in the light of the use of יצא הגורל, typical in legal contexts, instead of הפיל הגורל, encountered in eschatological contexts. The parallel in CD XIV.3–6 presenting 'a rule of the session for all the camps' seems to support the conclusion that the text may have referred to the ranking of members in an existing rather than in an eschatological community. This community, nevertheless, was seen as predestined and as fulfilling the will of God. The analysis of this document is still in its early stages, but the article by D. Hamidovic (2002) suggesting links with Psalm 135 and 4QWays of Righteousness (4Q421) gives promise of a lively discussion.

Editions and Further Reading

Alexander, P.S. and G. Vermes, '4QFour Lots (4Q279)', in P. S. Alexander and G. Vermes, *Qumran Cave 4.XIX: 4QSerekh Ha-Yaḥad and Two Related Texts* (DJD, 26; Oxford: Clarendon Press, 1998), pp. 217–23.

Hamidovic, D., '4Q279, *4QFour Lots*, une interpretation du Psaume 135 appartenant à 4Q421, 4QWays of Righteousness', *DSD* 9 (2002), pp. 166–86.

Metso, S., 'Constitutional Rules at Qumran', in P. W. Flint and J. C.VanderKam (eds), *The Dead Sea Scrolls After Fifty Years. A Comprehensive Assessment*, vol. 1 (Leiden: Brill, 1998), pp. 186–210 (esp. 205–207).

Rule (5Q13)

The manuscript 5Q13 was published under the name 'Une règle de la secte' by Milik in DJD, 3 (1962b: 181–83). Its contents, however, are quite diverse, and the original order of the fragments can no longer be determined. Fragments 1 and 2, which are the largest preserved, form a hymn or a prayer, where God is addressed in the second person singular and where his deeds in Israel's history are recounted. Fragment 4, on the other hand, bears similarities with the Community Rule: line 1 reads 'He shall stand before the *mebaqqer*'. The next two lines cite 1QS III.4–5, which denounce those who enter the covenant with an impure heart, and line 4 has a wording which coincides with 1QS II.19 'these things they shall do year after year', stating that the covenant ceremony is to be celebrated annually. Thus, either the writer copied sections from the Community Rule directly as a source, or the two documents share common sources.

L. H. Schiffman (1994: 132–43), who has analyzed 5Q13 more recently, identifies four distinct parts in the preserved text: The first part provides 'a retrospective review of the relationship of God to the biblical heroes continuing up through the founding of the sect': the second part gives a rule for 'the ritual for the annual covenant renewal and mustering': the third part 'indicates that those who are not members of the sect are prohibited from participation in the purification rituals which are part of the process': and the fourth part 'includes the confessional formula which is said as part of the atonement from sin, which, in the view of the sect, has to precede the attainment of ritual purity'. Schiffman concludes that overall, the text 'may function as a *serek*, a rule, for the conduct of the covenant renewal and the mustering ceremony of the Qumran sect' (1994: 133).

One Cave 4 manuscript of the Community Rule may provide an interesting parallel to the case of 5Q13. 4QS[h] has three fragments preserved, but only one of them (frg. 1) finds a parallel in 1QS. The text in the other two cannot be identified. Fragment 1 of 4QS[h] contains a parallel to 1QS III.4–5, which is the same phrase as the one in 5Q13, and like 5Q13, the two unidentified fragments in 4QS[h] bear characteristics of a hymn. Thus, a question arises whether 4QS[h] is a copy of the Community Rule at all, or a work simply citing the Community Rule. One has even to reckon with the possibility that the scant remains of 4QS[h] would represent a copy of 5Q13 with which it bears uncanny resemblance.

Editions and Further Reading

Milik, J. T., '5Q13. Une Règle de la Secte' in M. Baillet, J. T. Milik and R. de Vaux (eds), *Les 'Petites Grottes' de Qumran* (DJDJ, 3; Oxford: Clarendon Press, 1962), pp. 181–83, pls XXXIX–XL.

Schiffman, L. H., 'Sectarian Rule (5Q13)', in J. H. Charlesworth *et al.* (eds), *The Dead Sea Scrolls: Hebrew, Aramaic, and Greek Texts with English Translations*, vol. 1: *Rule of the Community and Related Documents* (Tübingen: J. C. B. Mohr [Paul Siebeck]; Louisville, KY: Westminster John Knox Press, 1994), pp. 132–43.

Chapter 7

FUNCTION OF RULE TEXTS IN THE ESSENE COMMUNITY

In the corpus of non-biblical scrolls found at Qumran, the rule texts represent one of the largest groups of manuscripts, and it is natural to ask how they might have functioned in the life of the Essene community and to what extent they reflect historical realities of the community. Considering their great variety and intricate textual relationships, these questions turn out to be very complex indeed – one needs only to point to the differences, but also to the similarities between, for example, the Community Rule, the Damascus Document and 4QMiscellaneous Rules (4Q265). Furthermore, not only are there differences between separate documents, there are also discrepancies even within single documents, and their redactional histories seem to complicate the situation even further.

Although manuscripts labelled as rule texts often include a variety of different genres, at the core of all these manuscripts are rules and regulations. It is natural to assume that the context from which rules emanated was the judicial proceedings of the community, that is, live situations in which oral discourse played a dominant role. Therefore, we need to look at the passages describing judicial proceedings in order to understand how legal traditions might have emerged and functioned in the community. In what follows we will examine the processes of generating, transmitting and recording legal traditions, and discuss the role oral decision-making could have played in the community's judicial proceedings. The intricate and complicated relationship between the oral and written forms of legal discourse has implications for understanding the tenuous link between the text and the historical reality behind it.

Processes of Generating Legal Traditions

There has been considerable discussion in regard to how the legal traditions were generated. Was scriptural exegesis the single source of Qumran legal traditions (Schiffman 1975: 19–21, 75–76; 2000: 131)? Did different communities operate differently? That is, did the community using the Damascus Document generate its legal traditions from scriptural exegesis while the community using the Community Rule based its traditions on some other source (Davies 1990: 38–39)? Or did a single community do both, differentiating between rules regarding the covenant, which were derived from the Torah, and rules for social organization, which were developed from the community's own practice (Weinfeld 1986: 71–76)?

Communal Study of the Law

As we look for material in the Qumran rule texts describing situations in which legal traditions in the Essene community were generated, two different types of communal gatherings stand out. The first involves communal study of the law:

> In the place where there are ten men let there not be lacking a man who studies the law day and night continually, one man being replaced by another. And the many shall watch together for a third of all the nights of the year to read the book, to study the ruling, and to pray together. (1QS VI.6–8)

For our discussion here, of interest is the wording at end of this passage: to read the book (לקרוא בספר), to study the law (לדרוש משפט), and to pray together (ולברך ביחד). This passage has been commented on by a number of scholars; the following observations are indebted in particular to M. Jaffee's discussion in his book *Torah in the Mouth* (2001). Jaffee calls attention to the distinction between verbs denoting kinds of study and their direct objects. The verb קרא, translated above as 'to read', actually designates recitation, that is, oral performance of a written text. Its object, הספר 'the Book', most likely denotes the biblical text, or more specifically the Pentateuch (note that in Josh. 1.8 the law of Moses is called ספר התורה; see also 4QMMT C 11). The verb דרש, translated above as 'to study', designates an act of exposition, but the question is: does its object משפט, here translated as 'ruling', also refer to the biblical text, as suggested, for example, by M. Knibb (1987: 117) and C. Hempel (2003: 66), or does it refer to some other entity? Jaffee puts the questions as follows: 'While it is clear that the recitation of the Book [הספר] is preliminary to the exposition of the Ruling [משפט], the relationship of these two acts remains unspecific. Is the Ruling exegetically derived from the Book, or is it an independent textual entity in its own right? In either event, is the Ruling a written document or an orally transmitted compendium of some sort?' (2001: 36).

In his answer to this question, Jaffee follows L. Schiffman's understanding of משפט as 'a technical term in CD and 1QS denoting behavioural prescriptions particular to the community. The Ruling [משפט], on this reading, is in some sense the preserved record of the periodic disclosure of things "hidden" from all Israel and "disclosed" to the Yaḥad in their collective textual studies "according to the Ruling of each time" (*lmspt 't w't*: ; CD 12:21)' [quoted from Jaffee 2001: 36]. Following this interpretation, Jaffee sees משפט as 'a source of teaching in its own right', and sees expounding [דרש] it as 'a matter of applying and extending the Ruling [משפט] itself'. Jaffee considers the evidence of successive revisions of communal regulations within CD and 1QS as supportive of this view, and concludes that 'this passage assumes the existence of an authoritative body of written texts related to, but separate from, the laws encoded in the Torah. It is the corpus of inner-communal "disclosures", rather than the unadorned scriptural text itself, that undergirds the specific form of life that distinguishes members of the community from those beyond its perimeter' (2001: 36).

Hempel's view, on the other hand, that משפט in the context of 1QS VI.6–7 refers to the Scriptures and not to the community's own laws, finds support in the terminological overlaps between our passage and some passages in Ezra-Nehemiah. According to Neh. 8.2, 8:

> They told the scribe Ezra to bring the book of the law of Moses, which the Lord had given to Israel. Accordingly, the priest Ezra brought the law before the assembly, both men and women and all who could hear with understanding... So they read from the book, from the law of God (ויקראו בספר בתורת האלהים), with interpretation (מפרש). They gave the sense (ושום שכל), so that the people understood the reading (ויבינו במקרא).

In Ezra 7.10, Ezra is described as follows: 'For Ezra had set his heart to study the law of the Lord (לדרוש את תורת יהוה), and to do it, and to teach the statutes and the ordinances in Israel (וללמד בישראל חק ומשפט)'. In the light of these parallels, the passage in 1QS VI.6–7 could be quite naturally interpreted as referring to communal study of biblical text. While it seems difficult to arrive at any conclusive interpretation of the passage, it seems plausible to me that the numerous pesharim found in the Qumran library were created in study sessions such as the one described in 1QS VI. Irrespective of how one understands the term משפט in this context, the passage in 1QS VI.6–7 gives evidence of communal recitation and study of written texts. Before commenting on this passage any further, I would like to turn to a few other passages in the Community Rule and the Damascus Document.

The Community's Sessions of Decision-Making

The second type of communal gathering in which legal traditions were created involves sessions of the communal decision-making. The session of the *rabbîm* is described in 1QS VI.8–13 as follows:

> This is the rule for a session of the many. Each (shall sit) according to his rank. The priests shall sit in the first seats, the elders in the second, and then the rest of all the people shall sit, each according to his rank. In the same order they shall be asked (ישאלו) for ruling (למשפט), or concerning any counsel (ולכול עצה) or matter which has to do with the many (ודבר אשר יהיה לרבים), each man offering his knowledge to the council of the community. No man shall interrupt his neighbour's words before his brother has finished speaking, or speak before one registered in rank before him. A man who is asked shall speak in his turn. In a session of the many no man shall say anything which is not approved by the many and, indeed, by the overseer of the many. Any man who has something to say to the many, but is not entitled to question the council of the community, shall stand on his feet and say, 'I have something to say to the many.' If they tell him to speak, he shall speak. (1QS VI.8–13; trans. Knibb)

A parallel to this passage can be found in the Damascus Document, where the rule for the meeting of the camps is recorded:

> The rule for the meeting of all the camps: they shall muster all of them by their names, the priests first, the levites second, the Israelites third, and the proselytes fourth. They shall be registered by their names each one after his brother: the priests first, the levites second, the Israelites third, and the proselytes fourth. And thus they shall sit and be consulted about everything (ישאלו לכל). (CD XIV.3–6)

Yet a third passage, found in 1QS IX.7, is of interest here. Its view of authority in the community somewhat differs from the one in 1QS VI:

Only the sons of Aaron shall rule in matters of justice (במשפט) and wealth (ובהון), and on their word the decision shall be taken (ועל פיהם יצא {ו} הגורל) with regard to every rule of the men of the community (לכול תכון אנשי היחד). (1QS IX.7; trans. Knibb)

According to Schiffman, the session of the *rabbîm* was a meeting 'at which they studied the Bible, explained it, and fixed the law' (1983: 15). But what catches my attention in these passages is the total lack of reference to any written text. The authority for decision-making is granted not to any book but rather to the *rabbim* (e.g., 1QS VI.8–13), members of the camps (CD XIV.3–6), or to the sons of Aaron (1QS IX.7). Thus, the possibility arises that the nature of the sessions described in these passages is fundamentally different from the biblical study sessions described in 1QS VI.6–7. The suggestion is reasonable that in the sessions of the community's decision making, the leading authorities did not resort to written regulations, but rather were guided by the oral tradition created and transmitted by the priestly members of the community. The authoritative form for community decision-making may well have been oral, not written. It is quite likely, of course, that the priests and community leaders who pronounced judgements in the sessions of the *rabbîm* were the same who participated in the study sessions of written documents as described in 1QS VI.6–7 and thus shared the same wealth of interpretive traditions. But the suggestion of the above passages, that in situations where community authority was exercised those traditions were present in oral rather than in written form, is highly significant for our understanding of the function of the compilations such as the Community Rule and the Damascus Document. We will return to this point later.

The view that biblical study sessions and sessions of communal decision making were different in nature is supported by the comparison of the vocabulary used in these passages. The verb שאל (niph.), 'to be asked', used in 1QS VI.9 and CD XIV.6, as well as the wording על פיהם 'according to their decision', literally 'according to their mouth' both point to the oral nature of the inquiry. As to the objects of this inquiry, 1QS VI.9 lists 'ruling' (משפט), 'any counsel' (כול עצה) and '(any) matter which has to do with the many' (דבר אשר יהיה לרבים);' CD XIV.6 uses the blanket term 'everything' (כל); and 1QS IX.7 lists 'justice' (משפט) and wealth (הון), and 'every rule of the men of the community' (כול תכון אנשי היחד). The fact that the word משפט is included in two of these lists is interesting in light of our earlier discussion of this term in 1QS VI.7, and speaks in favour of the view that at least in the current contexts of judicial meetings, it is used as a technical term for community's own laws, or 'behavioral prescriptions particular to the community' as suggested by Schiffman and Jaffee.

Authority of Legal Traditions

Even though a scholarly distinction between the different methods of generating halakah in the Essene community can be posited, the question remains as to whether the members of the community themselves would have made a distinction between the legal traditions derived from the study sessions of written texts, and those created as a result of oral rulings in judicial sessions. P. Davies (1990: 38–39) and M. Weinfeld (1986: 71–76) have suggested that in the Essene community, the rules governing communal life, such as penal regulations, rules of admission, and rules of community hierarchy were understood as fundamentally different from those derived from the Torah. A comparison between the Cave 1 and Cave 4 copies of the Community Rule indicates, however, that sometimes community rules, which originally were based on practical necessity, received scriptural authorization secondarily, when scriptural proof-texts were added to texts that originally lacked them. As examples of such rules can be mentioned rules stressing the need for separation from the outsiders and rules requiring an oath of those desiring to join the community. The community practices thus were based on practical exigencies, but at a secondary stage challenges may have been brought, and the practices may have required justification. This justification was given with the highest authority possible: the Scriptures.

This picture emerging from the comparison of Cave 1 and Cave 4 copies of the Community Rule corresponds to that of a recent study by H. Najman regarding the authorization of post-exilic political and legal practices in the traditions included in the writings of Ezra-Nehemiah. Najman demonstrates that an explicit Pentateuchal basis was not always necessary to ascribe some law or practice as 'Torah of Moses', but that legal innovations could be pseudonymously attributed to Moses as a means of authorization. She considers this as 'one of the main strategies through which Second Temple Judaism sought to authorize itself' (2000: 211). J. Baumgarten in his analysis of 4QOrdinances makes a similar comment: 'the peculiar method of rephrasing the biblical laws while inserting the elaborations of sectarian tradition serves to erase the distinction between biblical and non-biblical rules and to lend to all sectarian ordinances the aura of Mosaic authority' (1977a: 17).

The fact that we find a community tradition originally based on practical necessity later presented as derived from Scripture suggests that the community treated the laws of the Torah and community regulations as equally authoritative. This assumption is supported by the community's penal codes, in which the same punishment of permanent expulsion is applied on the one hand to the case of 'transgressing a word from the law of Moses presumptuously or negligently' (1QS VIII. 21–23), and equally on the other hand to the cases of 'slandering the *rabbîm*' (1QS VII.16–17, par. 4QD^e frg. 7 i 6–7), cases of 'making complaints about the authority of the community' (1QS VII.17), and cases of 'deviating from the fundamental principles of the community' after a full ten years of membership (1QS VII.18–25).

While it is certainly true that much of halakah was derived through scriptural exegesis, the view that it was the only avenue for generating halakic traditions may not be broad enough. The exigencies of communal life were an important source for new legal traditions, and their authorization by claims of Mosaic origin was a major strategy to guarantee adherence to practices protecting the community's integrity. Certain halakic traditions emerged independently from Scripture and were secondarily connected with the texts of the Torah; in some cases the 'exegetical hooks' discernible in the ancient writers' halakic discourse turn out to be the end result, not the starting point of the process. Schiffman and others have convincingly shown how halakic exegesis affected the behavioural patterns of the community, but the direction of the process was also the reverse: the community's behavioural patterns resulted in innovation of new halakah.

Transmission and Recording of Legal Traditions

As we consider the different setting in which legal traditions were created in the Essene community, we can find an interesting analogy in ancient rabbinic writings, although comparison of the rabbinic and Essene textual corpora involves many complexities. The Mishnaic rabbis kept developing new halakic material as court cases accumulated. It was not officially permitted to record the halakah in written form, and public discussions on the halakic decisions took place in oral form. However, privately preserved written records were produced for future guidance (cf. Mishnah Sanhedrin 4.2). The existence of such written records, as pointed out by J. Weingreen, is shown by Temura 14b, for example, that forbids the reciting of *oral* material from a *written* record. This provides 'clear evidence that what is designated as "oral" matter actually existed in written form' (1976: 79). Weingreen emphasizes that 'the adjective *oral* refers not to the means of preserving authoritative rabbinic legalistic materials, but only *to their circulation and transmission*' (1976: 79) Similarly, Jaffee stresses that 'the existence of an oral-literary tradition does not require an absence of literacy or writing' (2001: 8). 'The contents of the oral-literary tradition that had escaped written form was not perceived at all as an entity distinct from the book; rather, it was carried along within the orbit of the written text itself, as the performative tradition of its public exposition' (Jaffee 2001: 38).

In the light of this kind of textual evidence, we need to re-evaluate what we mean when we describe the Community Rule as a lawbook or rulebook. In the modern sense of the words, the term rulebook indicates a normative, legally binding set of written regulations that are prescriptive; but, as discussed above, in the judicial meetings recorded in the Community Rule there is never reference to written rules. The authority for decision-making is granted not to a written rulebook but rather to the *rabbîm* (e.g., 1QS VI.8–13) or to the sons of Aaron (1QS IX.7). Thus, the suggestion is reasonable that in the community's court proceedings, the leading authorities perhaps did not resort to written regulations, but rather were guided by the oral tradition created and transmitted by the priestly members of the community. The authoritative form for community decision-making may well have been oral, not written. If we assume that the purpose of the document was not to serve as a lawbook in the modern sense, but rather as a recording of different judicial decisions and a report of oral traditions, then the existence of contradictory regulations in compilations like the Community Rule is not so surprising. This kind of document would, of course, be of great significance nonetheless for educating the members of the community.

The community's responsibility in educating its new members is evident in passages describing the rules of admission into the community:

> Anyone who willingly offers himself from Israel to join the council of the community, the officer in charge (*paqîd*) at the head of the many shall examine him with respect to his insight and his deeds. If he is suited to the discipline, he shall admit him into the covenant that he may return to the truth and turn aside from all injustice, and shall instruct him in all the rules of the community (והבינהו בכול משפטי היחד) ... When he has completed a second year, he shall be examined on the authority of the many. If the decision is taken for him to draw near to the community, they shall register him in the order of his rank amongst his brothers, with respect to law, ruling, purity, and for pooling his wealth. His counsel and his judgment shall be available to the community. (1QS VI.13–15, 21–23; trans. Knibb)

In this passage, the necessity of study as a prerequisite for participation in community decision-making is likewise made very clear.

In addition to the officer in charge (*paqîd*), the wise leader (*maskîl*) had special responsibility in instructing the members of the community (see 1QS III.13; IX.18–21), and importantly, the Damascus Document states that the priest who musters at the head of the many shall be 'learned in the Book of Hagi and in all the ordinances of the law to pronounce them according to their rule' (לדברם כמשפטם; CD XIV.6–8).

Conclusion: Implications for Reconstructions of Community History

The Cave 4 material has preserved several cases of multiple manuscript copies of a single work. The copies are seldom fully identical; usually one can detect evidence of parallel editions and/or developing editorial stages. Potentially, these differences are very helpful in tracing historical developments in the groups responsible for creating and copying the manuscripts. But the situation is complicated by the fact that these documents, even in their earliest editorial stages, often prove to be compilations of different passages originating in different circles and different time periods, making it difficult to assign a single document to a particular group and to use that document as a reliable source of that group's ideas and practices at any given point of time.

On the basis of the comparison between the manuscripts of the Community Rule found in Caves 1, 4 and 5 it is clear that there never existed a single, legitimate and up-to-date version of the Community Rule that supplanted all other versions. The community continued copying the older and shorter form of the text even when a more extensive version was already available, just as happened with biblical manuscripts. The idea of a sole legitimate version is not supported by the internal indicators in the text, either: the earlier regulations were not omitted from the composition as new rules were created. The texts were 'cumulative' rather than 'up-to-date'. Therefore, the Community Rule, for example, contains two different sections originating at different times that describe the procedure of the admission of the new members and contains three different penal codes. The manuscripts also attest to the existence of contradictory practices, and it is practically impossible to determine which practice was followed at any particular time, although literary- and redaction-critical analysis can occasionally provide some indication as to the comparative age of each practice.

Thus, we have textual phenomena, such as parallel editions, developing editorial stages, and evidence of cross-influence between different documents, that pose challenges for those attempting direct historical reconstruction on the basis of rule texts found at Qumran. These textual phenomena become less puzzling if the function of these documents in the communal life of the Essenes is correctly understood. If we assume that the purpose of the document was not to serve as a prescriptive lawbook in the modern sense, but rather as a recording of different judicial decisions and a report of oral traditions, then the existence of contradictory regulations in compilations like the Community Rule is not so surprising. One should agree with Baumgarten regarding his many reservations in applying rabbinic categories to texts found at Qumran, but one should also recall his description of 'the topical rubrics in the legal section of the Damascus Document' as 'rudimentary manifestations of the methodology which ultimately resulted in the order of the Mishna' (1999: 58). The various processes that led to the emergence of legal traditions in the Essene community were likely not a sectarian anomaly but were part of the larger Jewish process of legal development and perhaps not so unlike those behind the emergence of the Mishnah.

Further Reading

Baumgarten, J. M., 'The Unwritten Law in the Pre-Rabbinic Period', in *Studies in Qumran Law* (Leiden: Brill, 1977), pp. 13–35 [= *JSJ* 3 (1972), pp. 7–29].

Davies, P. R., 'Halakhah at Qumran', in P. R. Davies and R. T. White (eds), *A Tribute to Geza Vermes: Essays on Jewish and Christian Literature and History* (JSOTSup, 100; Sheffield: JSOT Press, 1990), pp. 37–50.

Grossman, M. L., *Reading for History in the Damascus Document: A Methodological Study* (STDJ, 45: Leiden: Brill, 2002).

Hempel, C., *The Laws of the Damascus Document: Sources, Traditions and Redaction* (STDJ, 29; Leiden: Brill, 1998).

—'Interpretative Authority in the Community Rule Tradition', *DSD* 10 (2003), pp. 59–80.

Jaffee, M. S., *Torah in the Mouth: Writing and Oral Tradition in Palestinian Judaism, 200 BCE–400 CE* (Oxford: Oxford University Press, 2001).

Knibb, M. A., *The Qumran Community* (Cambridge Commentaries on Writings of the Jewish and Christian World 200 BC to AD 200, 2; Cambridge: Cambridge University Press, 1987).

Metso, S. 'In Search of the *Sitz im Leben* of the Community Rule', in D. W. Parry and E. Ulrich (eds), *The Provo International Conference on the Dead Sea Scrolls: Technological Innovations, New Texts, and Reformulated Issues* (STDJ, 30; Leiden: Brill, 1999), pp. 306–15.

—'Methodological Problems in Reconstructing History from Qumran Rule Texts', *DSD* 11 (2004), pp. 315–35.

—'Creating Community Halakhah', in P. W. Flint, E. Tov and J. C. VanderKam (eds), *Studies in the Hebrew Bible, Qumran, and the Septuagint: Presented to Eugene Ulrich* (Leiden: Brill, 2005), pp. 279–301.

Najman, H., 'Torah of Moses: Pseudonymous Attribution in Second Temple Writings', in C. A. Evans (ed.), *The Interpretation of Scripture in Early Judaism and Christianity: Studies in Language and Tradition* (JSPSup, 33; SSEJC, 7; Sheffield: Sheffield Academic Press, 2000), pp. 202–16.

Schiffman, L. H., *The Halakhah at Qumran* (SJLA, 16; Leiden: Brill, 1975).

—*Sectarian Law in the Dead Sea Scrolls: Courts, Testimony and the Penal Code* (Chico, CA: Scholars Press, 1983).

—'Halakhah and Sectarianism in the Dead Sea Scrolls', in T. H. Lim with L. W. Hurtado, A. G. Auld and A. Jack (eds), *The Dead Sea Scrolls in Their Historical Context* (Edinburgh: T&T Clark, 2000), pp. 123–42.

Talmon, S., 'Oral Tradition and Written Transmission, or the Heard and the Seen Word in Judaism of the Second Temple Period', *Jesus and the Oral Gospel Tradition* (JSNTSup, 64; Sheffield: Sheffield Academic Press, 1991), pp. 121–58.

Weingreen, J., *From Bible to Mishna: The Continuity of Tradition* (Manchester: Manchester University Press, 1976).

REFERENCES

Alexander, P. S.
    1996   'The Redaction-History of Serekh ha-Yaḥad: A Proposal', *RevQ* 17: 437–56.
Alexander, P. S. and G. Vermes.
    1998   *Qumran Cave 4,XIX: Serekh ha-Yaḥad and Two Related Texts*, (DJD, 26; Oxford: Clarendon Press).
Arata Mantovani, P.
    1983   'La stratificazione letteraria della *Regola della Communita*: A propositio di uno studio recente', *Henoch* 5: 69–91.
Bardtke, H.
    1974   'Literaturbericht über Qumran: VII Teil', *TRu* 38: 256–91.
Baumgarten, J. M.
    1976   'The Duodecimal Courts of Qumran, Revelation, and the Sanhedrin', *JBL* 95: 59–78.
    1977a   'The Unwritten Law in the Pre-Rabbinic Period', in *Studies in Qumran Law* (STDJ, 24; Leiden: Brill), pp. 13–35 (= *JSJ* 3 [1972]: 7–29).
    1977b   'On the Testimony of Women in 1QSa', in *Studies in Qumran Law* (STDJ, 24; Leiden: Brill), pp. 183–86 (= *JBL* 76 [1957]: pp. 266–69].
    1992   'The Cave 4 Versions of the Qumran Penal Code', *JJS* 43: 268–76.
    1996   *Qumran Cave 4.XIII: The Damascus Document (4Q266–273)* (DJD, 18; Oxford: Clarendon Press).
    1999   '4QMiscellaneous Rules (4Q265)', in J. Baumgarten *et al.*, *Qumran Cave 4.XXV: Halakhic Texts* (DJD, 35; Oxford: Clarendon Press) pp. 57–78, pls. V-VII.
Beall, T. S.
    1988   *Josephus' Description of the Essenes Illustrated by the Dead Sea Scrolls* (SNTSMS, 58; Cambridge: Cambridge University Press).
Becker, J.
    1964   *Das Heil Gottes: Heils- und Sündenbegriffe in den Qumrantexten und im Neuen Testament* (SUNT, 3; Göttingen: Vandenhoeck & Ruprecht).
Bockmuehl, M.
    1998   'Redaction and Ideology in the Rule of the Community (1QS/4QS),' *RevQ* 18: 541–60.
Bonani, G., M. Broshi, I. Carmi, S. Ivy, J. Strugnell and W. Wölfli
    1991   'Radiocarbon Dating of the Dead Sea Scrolls', *Atiqot* 20: 27–32.
Burrows, M., with J. C. Trever and W. H. Brownlee
    1951   *The Dead Sea Scrolls of St. Mark's Monastery*, vol. II, fasc. 2. *Plates and Transcription of the Manual of Discipline* (New Haven: American Schools of Oriental Research).
Charlesworth, J. H. and B. A. Strawn
    1996   'Reflections on the Text of Serekh ha-Yaḥad Found in Cave IV', *RevQ* 17: 403–35.

Charlesworth, J. H. and L. T. Stuckenbruck
    1994a   'Rule of the Congregation (1QSa)', in J. H. Charlesworth *et al.* (eds) *The Dead Sea Scrolls: Hebrew, Aramaic, and Greek Texts with English Translations*, vol. 1: *Rule of the Community and Related Documents* (Tübingen: J. C. B. Mohr [Paul Siebeck]; Louisville: Westminster John Knox Press), pp. 108–17.
    1994b   'Blessings', in J. H. Charlesworth *et al.* (eds) *The Dead Sea Scrolls: Hebrew, Aramaic, and Greek Texts with English Translations*, vol 1: *Rule of the Community and Related Documents* (Tübingen: J. C. B. Mohr [Paul Siebeck] Louisville: Westminster John Knox Press), pp. 119–31.

Collins, J. J.
    1995   *The Scepter and the Star: The Messiahs of the Dead Sea Scrolls and Other Ancient Literature* (New York: Doubleday).
    1997   *Apocalypticism in the Dead Sea Scrolls* (The Literature of the Dead Sea Scrolls, 1; London and New York: Routledge).
    2003   'Forms of Community in the Dead Sea Scrolls', in S. M. Paul *et al.* (eds), *Emanuel: Studies in Hebrew Bible, Septuagint, and Dead Sea Scrolls in Honor of Emanuel Tov* (Leiden: Brill), pp. 97–111.
    2006   'The Yaḥad and "The Qumran Community"', in C. Hempel and J. M. Lieu (eds), *Biblical Traditions in Transmission: Essays in Honour of Michael A. Knibb* (JSJSup 111; Leiden: Brill), pp. 81–96.

Cross, F.M.
    1994   'Paleographical Dates of the Manuscripts', in J. H. Charlesworth *et al.* (eds) *The Dead Sea Scrolls: Hebrew, Aramaic, and Greek Texts with English Translations*, vol. 1: *Rule of the Community and Related Documents* (Tübingen: J. C. B. Mohr [Paul Siebeck]; Louisville: Westminster John Knox Press), p. 57.

Davies, P. R.
    1990   'Halakhah at Qumran', in P. R. Davies and R. T. White (eds), *A Tribute to Geza Vermes. Essays on Jewish and Christian Literature and History* (JSOTSup, 100; Sheffield: JSOT Press), pp. 37–50.
    1994   'Communities in the Qumran Scrolls', *Proceedings of the Irish Biblical Association* 17: 55–68.

Delcor, M.
    1979   'Qumran. La Règle de la Communauté', *DBSup* 9 (Paris: Letouzey et Ané), pp. 851–57.

Dimant, D.
    1984   'Qumran Sectarian Literature', in M. E. Stone (ed.), *Jewish Writings of the Second Temple Period* (CRINT, 2:2; Assen: Van Gorcum; Philadelphia: Fortress), pp. 483–550.

Dohmen, C.
    1982   'Zur Gründung der Gemeinde von Qumran (1QS VIII-IX)', *RevQ* 11: 81–96.

Duhaime, J.
    2000   'Dualism', in L. H. Schiffman and J. C. VanderKam (eds), *Encyclopedia of the Dead Sea Scrolls*, vol. 1 (Oxford: Oxford University Press), pp. 215–20.

Dupont-Sommer, A.
    1952   'L'instruction sur les deux Esprits dans le "Manuel de Discipline"', *RHR* 142: 5–35.
    1953   *Nouveaux aperçus sur les manuscrits de la mer Morte* (A. Maisonneuve: Paris).

Eshel, E.
    2000   '4QRebukes Reported by the Overseer', in *Qumran Cave 4. XXVI Cryptic Texts and Miscellanea, part 1* (DJD, 36; Oxford: Clarendon Press), pp. 474–83 and pl. XXXII.

Falk, D. K.
    1998   *Daily, Sabbath, and Festival Prayers in the Dead Sea Scrolls* (STDJ, 27; Leiden: Brill).

Fitzmyer, J. A.
    1998   'Paul and the Dead Sea Scrolls', in P. W. Flint and J. C. VanderKam (eds), *The Dead Sea Scrolls After Fifty Years: A Comprehensive Assessment*, vol. 2 (Leiden: Brill), pp. 599–621.

García Martínez, F., E. J. C. Tigchelaar and A. S. van der Woude
    1998   '29. 11QFragment Related to Serekh ha-Yaḥad', in *Qumran Cave 11.II: 11Q2-18, 11Q20-31* (DJD, 23; Oxford: Clarendon), pp. 433–34, pl. L.

Garnet, P.
    1997   'Cave 4 MS Parallels to 1QS 5.1-7: Towards a *Serek* Text History', *JSP* 15: 67–78.

Guilbert, P.
    1958   'Deux écritures dans les colonnes VII et VIII de la Règle de la Communauté', *RevQ* 1: 199–212.

Hamidovic, D.
    2002   '4Q279, *4QFour Lots*, une interpretation du Psaume 135 appartenant à 4Q421, 4QWays of Righteousness', *DSD* 9: 166–86.

Harlow, D. C.
    2003   'The Dead Sea Scrolls and the New Testament', in J. C. Dunn and J. W. Rogerson (eds), *Eerdmans Commentary on the Bible* (Grand Rapids, MI: Eerdmans), pp. 1577–86.

Hempel, C.
    1995   'Who Rebukes in *4Q477*?' *RevQ* 16: 655–56.
    1996   'The Early Essene Nucleus of 1QSa', *DSD* 3: 253–69.
    1997   The Penal Code Reconsidered', in M. Bernstein, F. García Martínez, and J. Kampen (eds), *Legal Texts and Legal Issues: Proceedings of the Second Meeting of the International Organization for Qumran Studies, Cambridge 1995* (Leiden: Brill), pp. 337–48.
    1999   'Community Structures in the Dead Sea Scrolls: Admission, Organization, Disciplinary Procedures', in P. W. Flint and J. C. VanderKam (eds), *The Dead Sea Scrolls After Fifty Years. A Comprehensive Assessment*, vol. 2 (Leiden: Brill), pp. 67–92.
    2000   *The Damascus Texts* (Companion to the Qumran Scrolls, 1; Sheffield: Sheffield Academic Press)
    2003   'Interpretative Authority in the Community Rule Tradition', *DSD* 10: 59–80.

Hempel, J.
    1963   'Die Stellung des Laien in Qumran', in H. Bardtke (ed.), *Qumran-Probleme: Vorträge des leipziger Symposions über Qumran-Probleme vom 9. bis 14. Oktober 1961* (Berlin: Akademie-Verlag), pp. 193–215.

Jaffee, M. S.
    2001   *Torah in the Mouth: Writing and Oral Tradition in Palestinian Judaism. 200 BCE-400 CE* (Oxford: Oxford University Press).

Knibb, M. A.
    1987   *The Qumran Community* (Cambridge Commentaries on Writings of the Jewish and Christian World 200 BC to AD 200, 2; Cambridge: Cambridge University Press).
    2000   'Rule of the Community', in L. H. Schiffman and J. C. VanderKam (eds), *Encyclopedia of the Dead Sea Scrolls* (Oxford: Oxford University Press), pp. 793–77.

Kobelski, P. J.
    1981   *Melchizedek and Melchiresha'* (Washington, DC: Catholic Biblical Association).
Koenen, K.
    1993   'שָׂכַל', *ThWAT* 7: 782–95.
Kugler, R. A.
    1996   'A Note on 1QS 9.14: The Sons of Righteousness or the Sons of Zadok?' *DSD* 3: 315-20.
Kuhn, H.-W.
    1966   *Enderwartung und gegenwärtiges Heil* (Göttingen: Vandenhoeck & Ruprecht).
Kuhn, K.-G.
    1952   'Die Sektenschrift und die iranische Religion', *ZTK* 49: 296–316.
Leaney, A. R. C.
    1966   *The Rule of Qumran and Its Meaning: Introduction, Translation and Commentary* (London: S.C.M. Press).
Licht, J.
    1965   *Megillat has-Serakim: The Rule Scroll: A Scroll from the Wilderness of Judaea: 1QS, 1QSa, 1QSb: Text, Introduction and Commentary* (Jerusalem: Bialik Institute).
Lieberman, S.
    1952   'The Discipline in the So-called Dead Sea Manual of Discipline', *JBL* 71: 199–206.
Magness, J.
    2002   *The Archaeology of Qumran and the Dead Sea Scrolls* (Studies in the Dead Sea Scrolls and Related Literature; Grand Rapids, MI: Eerdmans).
Martin, M.
    1958   *The Scribal Character of the Dead Sea Scrolls, I-II* (Louvain: Publications universitaires).
Medico, H. E. del,
    1951   *Deux manuscrits hébreux de la Mer Morte* (Paris: Librairie orientaliste P. Geuthner).
Metso, S.
    1993   'The Primary Results of the Reconstruction of 4QS^e', *JJS* 44: 303–308.
    1997   *The Textual Development of the Qumran Community Rule* (STDJ, 21; Leiden: Brill).
    2000a   'The Relationship between the Damascus Document and the Community Rule', in J. M. Baumgarten, E. G. Chazon and A. Pinnick (eds), *The Damascus Document: A Centennial of Discovery. Proceedings of the Third International Symposium of the Orion Center, 4–8 February, 1998* (STDJ, 34; Leiden: Brill), pp. 85–93.
    2000b   'The Redaction of the Community Rule', in L. H. Schiffman, E. Tov and J. C. VanderKam (eds), *Proceedings of the International Congress 'The Dead Sea Scrolls: Fifty Years After Their Discovery'* (Jerusalem: Israel Exploration Society/Shrine of the Book Museum, Israel), pp. 377–84.
    2002   'Biblical Quotations in the Community Rule', in E. D. Herbert and E. Tov (eds), *The Bible as Book: The Hebrew Bible and the Judaean Desert Discoveries* (London: The British Library and Oak Knoll Press in association with The Scriptorium, Center for Christian Antiquities), pp. 81–92.
    2005   'Creating Community Halakhah', in P. W. Flint, E. Tov and J. C. VanderKam (eds), *Studies in the Hebrew Bible, Qumran, and the Septuagint: Presented to Eugene Ulrich* (Leiden: Brill), pp. 279–301.

2006   Whom Does the Term *Yaḥad* Identify?', in C. Hempel and J. Lieu (eds), *Biblical Traditions in Transmission: Essays in Honour of Michael A. Knibb* (JSJSup, 111; Leiden: Brill), pp. 213–235.

Milik, J. T.
1955   'Recueil des Bénédictions (1QSb)', in D. Barthélemy and J. T. Milik (eds), *Qumran Cave I* (DJD, 1; Oxford: Clarendon), pp. 118–30, pls. XXV–XXIX.
1959   *Ten Years of Discovery in the Wilderness of Judaea* (trans. J. Strugnell [*Dix ans de découvertes dans le Désert de Juda*; Paris: Cerf, 1957]; SBT, 26; London: SCM Press).
1960   'Texte des variantes des dix manuscrits de la Règle de la Communauté trouvés dans la Grotte 4: Recension de P.Wernberg-Moeller, The Manual of Discipline', *RB* 67: 410–16.
1962   '5Q11. Règle de la Communauté', in M. Baillet, J. T. Milik and R. de Vaux, *Les 'Petites Grottes' de Qumrân* (DJDJ, 3; Oxford: Clarendon), pp. 180–81, pl. XXXVIII.
1962b   '5Q13. Une Règle de la Secte', in M. Baillet, J. T. Milik and R. de Vaux, *Les 'Petites Grottes' de Qumrân* (DJDJ, 3; Oxford: Clarendon, 1962), pp. 181–83 + pls XXXIX–XL.
1976   *The Books of Enoch: Aramaic Fragments of Qumrân Cave 4* (Oxford: Clarendon).
1977   'Numérotation des feuilles des rouleaux dans le scriptorium de Qumrân (Planches X et XI)', *Semitica* 27: 75–81.

Murphy-O'Connor, J.
1969   'La genèse littéraire de la Règle de la Communauté', *RB* 76: 528–49.
1986   'The Judean Desert', in R. A. Kraft and G. W. E. Nickelsburg (eds), *Early Judaism and Its Modern Interpreters* (Atlanta: Scholars Press), pp. 119–56.

Najman, H.
2000   'Torah of Moses: Pseudonymous Attribution in Second Temple Writings', in C. A. Evans (ed.), *The Interpretation of Scripture in Early Judaism and Christianity: Studies in Language and Tradition* (JSPSup, 33; SSEJC, 7; Sheffield: Sheffield Academic Press), pp. 202–16.

Nitzan, B.
1994   *Qumran Prayer and Religious Poetry* (trans. J. Chipman; STDJ, 12; Leiden: Brill), pp. 125–39.

Nötscher, F.
1960   'Heiligkeit in den Qumranschriften', *RevQ* 2: 315–44.

Pfann, S. J.
2000   '4Q249a-i: 4Qpap CryptA Serekh ha-"Edah[a-j]', in *Qumran Cave 4. XXVI: Cryptic Texts* (DJD, 36; Oxford: Clarendon Press]), pp. 515–74, pls. XXXV–XXXVII.

Philonenko, M.
1995   'La doctrine qoumrânienne des deux esprits: Ses origines iraniennes et ses prolongements dans le judaïsme essénien et le christianisme antique', in G. Widengren, A. Hultgård and M. Philonenko, *Apocalyptique iranienne et dualisme qoumrânien* (Reserches intertestamentaires, 2; Paris: Maisonneuve), pp. 163–211.

Ploeg, J. van der
1951   'Le 'Manuel de Discipline' des rouleaux de la Mer Morte', *BO* 8: 113–26.

Pouilly, J.
1976   *La Règle de la Communauté: Son evolution littéraire* (Cahiers de la Revue Biblique, 17; Paris: Gabalda).

Priest, J. F.
    1962   'Mebaqqer, Paqid, and the Messiah', *JBL* 81: 55–61.

Puech, É.
    1979a   'Remarques sur l'écriture de 1QS VII-VIII', *RevQ* 10: 35–43.
    1979b   'Recension: J.Pouilly, La Règle de la Communauté de Qumran: Son evolution littéraire', *RevQ* 10: 103–11.
    1993   *La croyance des Esséniens en la vie future: immortalité, résurrection, vie éternelle? Histoire d'une croyance dans le judaïsme ancien. II: Les donnés qumraniennes et classiques* (Études bibliques, Novelle série, 22; Paris: Gabalda).

Qimron, E. and J. H. Charlesworth, with an Appendix by F. M. Cross
    1994   'Cave IV Fragments (4Q255-264 = 4QS MSS A-J)', in J. H. Charlesworth *et al.* (eds) *The Dead Sea Scrolls: Hebrew, Aramaic, and Greek Texts with English Translations*, vol. 1: *Rule of the Community and Related Documents* (Tübingen: J. C. B. Mohr [Paul Siebeck]; Louisville: Westminster John Knox Press), pp. 53–103.

Reed, S.
    1996   'Genre, Setting, and Title of 4Q477', *JJS* 47: 147–48.

Schiffman, L. H.
    1975   *The Halakhah at Qumran* (SJLA, 16; Leiden: Brill).
    1983   *Sectarian Law in the Dead Sea Scrolls: Courts, Testimony and the Penal Code* (BJS, 33; Chico, CA: Scholars Press,).
    1989   *The Eschatological Community of the Dead Sea Scrolls: A Study of the Rule of the Congregation* (Atlanta: Scholars Press).
    1994   'Sectarian Rule (5Q13)', in J. H. Charlesworth *et al.* (eds), *The Dead Sea Scrolls: Hebrew, Aramaic, and Greek Texts with English Translations*, vol. 1: *Rule of the Community and Related Documents* (Tübingen: J. C. B. Mohr [Paul Siebeck]; Louisville: Westminster John Knox Press), pp. 132–43.
    2000   'Halakhah and Sectarianism in the Dead Sea Scrolls', in T. H. Lim with L. W. Hurtado, A. G. Auld, and A. Jack (eds), *The Dead Sea Scrolls in Their Historical Context* (Edinburgh: T&T Clark), pp. 123–42.

Schuller, E.
    1999   '4Q433a. 4QpapHodayot-like Text B', in E. Chazon *et al.*, *Qumran Cave 4. XX: Poetical and Liturgical Texts*, part 2 (DJD, 29; Oxford: Clarendon), pp. 237–45, pl. XV.

Stegemann, H.
    1998   *The Library of Qumran: On the Essenes, Qumran, John the Baptist, and Jesus* (orig. *Die Essener, Qumran, Johannes der Täufer und Jesus: Ein Sachbuch* [Freiburg: Herder, 1993]; Grand Rapids, MI: Eerdmans; Leiden: Brill).

Steudel, A.
    1992   'אחרית הימים in the Texts from Qumran', *RevQ* 16: 225–46.

Sutcliffe, E. F.
    1959   'The First Fifteen Members of the Qumran Community: A Note on 1QS 8:1 ff.', *JSS* 4: 134–38.

Tigchelaar, E. J. C.
    2000   'A Newly Identified 11QSerekh ha-Yaḥad Fragment (11Q29)?', in L. H. Schiffman, E. Tov and J. C. VanderKam (eds), *The Dead Sea Scrolls: Fifty Years After Their Discovery. Proceedings of the Jerusalem Congress, July 20-25, 1997* (Jerusalem: Israel Exploration Society in cooperation with the Shrine of the Book Museum, Israel), pp. 285–92.

Tov, E.
    2004   *Scribal Practices and Approaches Reflected in the Texts Found in the Judean Desert* (STDJ, 54; Leiden: Brill).

Ulrich, E.
    1979   '4QSam^c: A Fragmentary Manuscript of 2 Samuel 14–15 from the Scribe of the Serek Hay-yahad (1QS)', *BASOR* 235: 1–25.
    2002   'The Absence of "Sectarian Variants" in the Jewish Scriptural Scrolls found at Qumran', in E. D. Herbert and E. Tov (eds), *The Bible as Book: The Hebrew Bible and the Judaean Desert Discoveries* (London: The British Library and Oak Knoll Press in association with The Scriptorium, Center for Christian Antiquities), pp. 179–95.

VanderKam, J. C.
    1994a   'Messianism in the Scrolls', in E. Ulrich and J. VanderKam (eds), *The Community of the Renewed Covenant* (Notre Dame, IN: University of Notre Dame Press), pp. 211–34.
    1994b   *The Dead Sea Scrolls Today* (Grand Rapids: Eerdmans).

Vaux, R. de
    1973   *Archaeology and the Dead Sea Scrolls* (Oxford: Oxford University Press, rev. edn).

Vermes, G.
    1991   'Preliminary Remarks on Unpublished Fragments of the Community Rule from Qumran Cave 4', *JJS* 42: 250–55.
    2004   *The Complete Dead Sea Scrolls in English* (London: Penguin Books, rev. edn).

Weinfeld, M.
    1986   *The Organizational Pattern and the Penal Code of the Qumran Sect. A Comparison with Guilds and Religious Associations of the Hellenistic-Roman Period* (NTOA, 2; Göttingen: Vandenhoeck & Ruprecht).

Weingreen, J.
    1976   *From Bible to Mishna: The Continuity of Tradition* (Manchester: Manchester University Press).

Weise, M.
    1961   *Kultzeiten und kultischer Bundesschluss in der 'Ordensregel' vom Toten Meer* (SPB, 3; Leiden: Brill).

Wernberg-Møller, P.
    1957   *The Manual of Discipline Translated and Annotated with an Introduction* (STDJ, 1; Leiden: Brill).
    1961   'A Reconsideration of the Two Spirits in the Rule of the Community (I Q Serek III,13–IV,26)', *RevQ* 3: 413–41.

INDEXES

INDEX OF REFERENCES

BIBLE

OTHER ANCIENT REFERENCES

1QS (cont.)		VI.9	31, 66	VIII	12, 21–3
V.15–VII.25	15	VI.10–13	3	VIII.1–IX.26	16
V.15b–VII.25	16	VI.10	31, 32	VIII.1–IX.26a	12
V.15	10	VI.11–12	32, 46	VIII.1–IX.11	12
V.15b	10	VI.12	37	VIII.1–16	15
V.16–19	57	VI.13–23	29, 57	VIII.1–15a	7, 13
V.16b–19a	42, 43	VI.13b–23	10, 11, 28–	VIII.1–13a	13
V.17	57		30	VIII.1–12	33
V.20b–VI.1a	11	VI.13–15	69	VIII.1–8	33, 57
V.20b–VI.1b	10	VI.13	32	VIII.1–7a	16
V.20b–25a	10	VI.14–15	36	VIII.1–2	21
V.20b–24	28–30	VI.14	37	VIII.1	30, 32, 46
V.20–23	28, 29	VI.16–23	46	VIII.2	22
V.21	46	VI.16–18	11	VIII.4	15, 23, 32
V.22–24	9	VI.16–17	47, 53	VIII.4b	12
V.23–24	29	VI.16	32, 60	VIII.5	18
V.24–VI.1	47, 58	VI.18–23	69	VIII.7b–12a	16
V.24b–VI.1a	11	VI.18–21	23	VIII.10–12	16
V.25b–VI.1b	10	VI.18	46, 60	VIII.10b–12a	13
V.25	10	VI.20–21	47	VIII.10	22, 23, 57
V.26	9	VI.20	37, 53	VIII.12–16	13, 57
VI–VII	35	VI.22–25	12	VIII.12b–16a	43
VI	13, 31, 65	VI.22	60	VIII.12	15, 32
VI.1–8	31, 32	VI.24–VII.25	12, 33, 34	VIII.12b	12, 16
VI.1b–8a	10	VI.24–25	33, 46	VIII.13b–14	13
VI.1c–8a	30	VI.25–27	56	VIII.13	22
VI.1–7	11, 30	VI.25	34, 56	VIII.14	57
VI.1c–7a	31, 32	VII–IX	4	VIII.15–IX.11	17, 18
VI.1–4	5	VII–VIII	18	VIII.15b–IX.11	5, 13, 30
VI.1–3	9, 30	VII	12	VIII.15b–19	16
VI.1b–2a	10	VII.2	32	VIII.15a	16
VI.2	30, 31	VII.3–4	56	VIII.16–IX.2	15
VI.3–5	9, 53	VII.4–5	34	VIII.16b–IX.2	33
VI.3–4	30	VII.5b–8	34	VIII.16b–19	13, 33, 34
VI.3	31	VII.5	56	VIII.16b–18a	33
VI.4–6	47, 53	VII.8–21	35	VIII.16	46
VI.4	31	VII.8–9	59	VIII.18b	33
VI.5	31	VII.8	35, 56	VIII.19	33
VI.6–23	29	VII.9–10	34	VIII.20–IX.2	13, 16
VI.6–8	22, 64	VII.10	56	VIII.21–23	67
VI.6–7	64–6	VII.12	18	VIII.21b–23a	33, 34
VI.7	11, 66	VII.14–15	56	VIII.21	33
VI.7b–8a	31	VII.14	35	IX–XI	16
VI.8–13	31, 32, 53,	VII.15–16	34	IX–X	5
	65, 66, 68	VII.15	34	IX	12
VI.8b–13	31, 32	VII.16–17	67	IX.2	33
VI.8b–13a	11, 30	VII.18–25	67	IX.3–11	13, 16
VI.8–9	60	VII.18–19	6	IX.3	13, 15, 32,
VI.8	31, 55, 65	VII.22–24	32		46
VI.8b	11	VIII–IX	12, 15, 16,	IX.5	33
VI.9–12	30		21, 30, 32